SEA GATE
REMEMBERED

SEA GATE
REMEMBERED

*New York City's
First Gated Community*

Arnold Rosen

Library of Congress Number: 2003095526
ISBN :   Hardcover   1-4134-2436-8
                Softcover   1-4134-2435-X

This book was printed in the United States of America.

Cover photograph courtesy of the Brooklyn Public Library (Brooklyn Collection)
- Grand Army Plaza, Brooklyn, New York.

To order additional copies of this book, contact:
Xlibris Corporation
1-888-795-4274
www.Xlibris.com
Orders@Xlibris.com
19577

CONTENTS

For my Beloved Marylyn,
And the joys of my life, Paul, Suzy, and Cyrus

Also by Arnold Rosen

Machine Transcription, published by Media Systems, Inc. (A subsidiary of Harcourt Brace Jovanovich, Inc.), 1975.

Word Processing, published by Prentice-Hall, Inc., 1977, 1982.

Word Processing Keyboarding Applications & Exercises, published by John Wiley & Sons, Inc., 1981, 1985.

Language Skills for Transcription, published by Media systems, Inc. (A subsidiary of Harcourt Brace Jovanovich, Inc.), 1981.

Administrative Procedures for the Electronic Office, published by John Wiley & Sons, Inc., 1982, 1985.

Getting the Most out of Your Word Processor, published by Prentice-Hall, Inc., 1983.

Information Processing: Keyboarding Applications & Exercises, published by John Wiley & Sons, Inc., 1985.

Telecommunications, published by Harcourt Brace Jovanovich, Inc., 1987.

Office Automation and Information Systems, published by Merrill Publishing Co., 1987.

Desktop Publishing: Applications & Exercises, published by Harcourt Brace Jovanovich, Inc., 1989.

The Word Perfect Book, published by Harcourt Brace Jovanovich, Inc., 1989.

Using PFS: First Publisher (served as technical editor), published by Que Corporation, 1990.

Quick Reference Guide to Pagemaker 4.0—IBM Version, published by Wm. C. Brown, Publishers, 1992.

Quick Reference Guide to Coreldraw, 3.0, published by Wm. C. Brown, Publishers, 1993.

Quick Reference Guide to Word Perfect 5.1, published by Wm. C. Brown, Publishers, 1993

Quick Reference Guide to Word Perfect for Windows, published by Wm. C. Brown, Publishers, 1993.

Quick Reference Guide to Lotus 1-2-3, Version 2.3, published by Wm. C. Brown, Publishers, 1993.

Quick Reference to Harvard Graphics, published by Wm. C. Brown, Publishers, 1993.

Quick Reference Guide to Pagemaker, Macintosh Version, published by Wm. C. Brown, Publishers, 1993.

ACKNOWLEDGEMENTS

The decision to write this book was an easy one. Before a single keystroke was transmitted to my computer, I had the encouragement and inspiration of so many wonderful people. The foundation of my success in preparing this book was the support and tolerance of someone closest to me—my beloved Marylyn. It was she who tolerated a room full of computers, books, papers, and long periods of isolated work. She offered me the love and encouragement I needed to carry me through the rigors of writing. To you, Marylyn, I say thank you.

I can't say enough about my childhood friend, writer and former editor of the *Potomac Review*, Eli Flam. We grew up together as denizens of the Riviera basketball courts. He read the entire manuscript and I am indebted to him for his meticulous proofreading, guidance and suggestions throughout the writing of this book. Bobby Browne-Cramer, another talented writer and friend, read the first draft pages of the manuscript and was kind enough to offer her critical evaluation and guidance.

Thanks to all the gracious ex-Sea Gaters who responded to my request to submit their questionnaires, shared their memories and some of their old photos:

Ted Arenson, Bill Backalenick, Theda Backalenick-Frank, David Buxbaum, Paul Berg, Arlene Bergen-Greenfield, Herbert Blecker, Lenore Boni-DePillo, Don Brenner, Darryl Dworman, Marilyn Ferber-Kopp, Laurie Frankel-Feuerman, Gene Goldberg, Leonard Fisher, Al Goldstein, Stanley Greenstein, Harriet Harnett-Marks, Joel Harnett, Bob Harnick, Judy Levine-Natter, Diane Lipson-Altman, Naomi Lipson-Hochman, Eddie Mann, Henry Marcus, Lee Meyerhoff, Kadish Millet, Marvin Minoff, Irene Needle-Halpern, Florence Needle-Weingram, Richard Oberfield, Gene Rifkin, Don Robins, Harold Rosen, Diana Rubinstein-Wiener, Ralph Sevuch, Rhoda Shapiro-Montella, Morris Shorofsky, Sheldon and Walter Spodek, Gloria Steinberg-Gerst, Jerry Stern, Robert Tannen, Martha Warshaw—and to Coney Islanders: Stanley Davis, Bob Greenwald, Phil Horn, Sidney Krimsky, Steve Jackel, and Mort Weiner.

I am especially grateful to the following people who allowed me to visit with them and record their memories on tape: Bruce Akrongold, Sal Argano, Kalman Bergen, Irma Freedman-Most, Martha Goldstein-Reinken, Evalyn Greenstein-Krown, Melvin (Sonny) Krown, Pearl Hornreich, Donald Nier, Donald Picker, Lou Powsner, Pete Spanakos, Noel Schwartz, Teri Seidman, Lenny Wachs, and Mickey and Carol Weinshanker.

Additional appreciation is extended to Lisa Cosme-Hernandez, community manager of the Sea Gate Association; Sean Ashby of the Brooklyn Historical Society; June Koffi of the Brooklyn Public Library, Grand Army Plaza (Brooklyn Collection); Richard Cox of the Harbor Defense Museum, U.S. Army Garrison, Fort Hamilton, and Barbara Dreher, K.C. Pritchard and Peg Libby of the West Hempstead, New York Public Library. The wonderful trolley photos were made available through the generosity of transit authority veterans, Don Harold and Bob Presbrey.

My work with the editorial and production staff at Xlibris has been a pleasurable experience. They have been most supportive and accessible at every stage of the publication process.

Lastly, I would be remiss if I didn't extend a special "thank you" to a beautiful and courageous lady, Barbara Harnett-Weil. She invited me to her home in Stamford, Connecticut, and we sat for a wonderful two-hour interview. She not only supplied me with precious narratives about her life in Sea Gate, but referred me to other Sea Gaters who contributed enriching narratives as well. I called Barbara a few days after the interview to express my appreciation. Her response was, "The pleasure was all mine. Your interview evoked such wonderful memories and enabled me to relive some of my glorious childhood years. For that I thank you."

If I have forgotten anyone, please let me know. I will buy you a day pass to the Sea Gate Beach, lunch at the Riviera, apologize profusely and thank you in person.

PREFACE

When I retired from teaching and writing twenty college textbooks, I vowed to relax and promised myself not to write any more books. Never say "*never*" again. Over the past several years I have had the pleasure of reconnecting with some of my Sea Gate childhood friends, many of whom I have not seen or talked with for over fifty years. Through e-mails, telephone conversations, visits, and reunion gatherings, we shared stories of growing up in Sea Gate and the wonderful memories of family and friends. The magnificent beach, the games we played, the somber war years, and the ferocious storms, brought to mind indelible recollections of our youth. After our reminiscing, my friends would ask, "When are you going to write that in a book?" The idea became more and more intriguing.

As a result, *Sea Gate Remembered: New York City's First Gated Community* was born. This book spans Sea Gate's rich and colorful history, from its earliest days—even before the first settlers arrived from Europe—to the present.

My Rationale

Years ago, the demographics of neighborhoods were often

cyclical. Generations were born, raised and married without moving from the old hometown. Now it's the rule, and not the exception, that finds families scattered across the country and convening only for standard rites of passage: births, weddings, funerals, and religious holidays. But what has remained constant is *nostalgia*—the continual power of early memories.

Sea Gate Remembered fills the gaps between the then and now for the thousands of present and former residents who have called this unique community home. Consider it a "reunion in print," which would also be a bridge back to the "good old days" as well as a document for subsequent generations—the offspring of former Sea Gaters who, in our ever-changing world, would welcome a personal insight to the way we were.

My greatest resource for the book came from memories and recollections of ex-Sea Gaters who grew up there in the 1930s, '40s and early '50s. Their stories—often wistful, pointed, and humorous—evoke this earlier era. With tape recorder in hand, I visited Sea Gaters in their homes; I met others in diners over lunch, and what a workout the phone got. So many good folks returned questionnaires and contributed narratives of their Sea Gate days. To capture these fascinating oral histories, I devoted the entire chapter 4, "I Remember"; it combines their photos and narratives. I found their stories compelling, and they're scattered throughout the book.

As a kid in Sea Gate, I loved photography and taking pictures. I used a Kodak box camera and developed my own photos in the basement of my home on Surf Avenue. I became obsessed to own a movie camera. When I asked my father to buy me one, he said, "If you want it, why don't you get a summer job and earn it yourself?" I filled out working papers at Mark Twain Junior High School in 1946, got a summer job in Coney Island and earned enough to buy a Revere movie camera and projector, which I purchased at Weiner's Photo Store on Mermaid Avenue when I was fourteen years old. The movie camera went with me almost everywhere I went. I especially took pictures on the beach and the basketball court at "the Riviera" and the softball field between Surf and Mermaid Avenues. "Freeze-frame" photos from this trove, together with some earlier still photos, bring added life to the stories. Also included in the book are photographs, maps, drawings, and memorabilia from ex-Sea Gaters plus archival photos from the Sea Gate Association, the Brooklyn Historic Society, and the Brooklyn Public Library.

I have striven to capture the flavor of the Sea Gate you grew up in or heard so much about—or perhaps this is new terrain for you. May you enjoy the trip.

INTRODUCTION

At Brooklyn's southwesternmost point, the conjoined Gravesend Bay and Lower New York Bay ripple lightly in the ample morning view through Pete Spanakos's dining room window. The lordly sweep of the Verrazano Bridge commands the middle distance, connecting Brooklyn on the right with Staten Island on the left by arcing over the heavily trafficked narrows. Some fifty years ago, I remember, as a beach-struck Sea Gate teenager I canoed the many miles from Beach One north through the narrows to the freighter-filled Gowanus Canal and back, with lifeguard Joe, a look-alike for bodybuilder Charles Atlas, a steady taskmaster in the stern. As kids we saw ocean liners like the *Normandie* and the *Queen Mary* steam regally toward the narrows and the docks of Manhattan beyond. I've read that when ex-President Teddy Roosevelt returned in 1910 from a much-ballyhooed African safari, celebrations began off Sea Gate, where the liner he was on "shot out of the fog" and cannon from forts and warships in the harbor were readied to fire salutes.

Alongside Pete, I stare with Arnie Rosen and Ted Arenson, friends from the old days, at the unceasing flow of traffic across the Verrazano Bridge. This view is new for all of us, visiting Ocean View Avenue for the first time since we left Sea Gate as teenagers in the early '50s; the bridge was opened in 1964. I wonder what

Giovanni Verrazano, who came in 1524, looking for a northwest passage to Asia, would say at the sight. Or Henry Hudson, who anchored nearby on the same mission in 1609. Much less latter-day architect-playboy Stanford White, who designed Sea Gate's late, luxurious Atlantic Yacht Club.

Spanakos, who became Sea Gate's informal historian soon after moving here from Brooklyn's Red Hook in 1967, exclaimed, "I love it here! So much to see, and the sunsets by the bridge are beautiful." The former counselor and national amateur bantamweight boxing champ jabs toward the tidy fishing boat dallying a few hundred yards off the bulkhead, lines in the water. "Now," he says, "you get striped bass, bluefish, flounder, weak fish and fluke—everything, since the water was cleaned up. Lately, though," he adds, "blue claw and horseshoe crabs haven't been seen as much."

It's November. The in-ground pool between house and bulkhead is covered. Spanakos built it when hypodermic needles washed in too often, presumably after use for shooting drugs. Now, he says, they're absent, and you can swim in the water.

A predecessor to the ten-foot-high cyclone fence a few hundred yards to the right, laced on top with loops of barbed wire, was originally erected in 1899 to separate Sea Gate from Coney Island. The fence became embroiled in the Bay View War of the late 1990s, and it still doesn't keep everybody out, especially at low tide. One day, Pete recalls, he looked down from the bulkhead and saw a naked young twosome going at it hot and heavy on the beach. Thinking of his kids, he hustled down the stairs of his pier, tapped the man on a shoulder and told the pair to leave. The man, in a Russian accent, took exception; in America he was entitled to freedom. The woman, though, put on her string bikini, and Pete didn't have to call the private Sea Gate police—officially labelled "peace officers."

In the living room Pete points to a baby grand piano (purchased from the estate of Dr. Radetsky) in a corner. Beverly

Sills played on it when she lived in Sea Gate as young Bubbles Silverman. "Did the future opera star play the hit radio commercial she recorded for Rinso, king of soap flakes, on this piano?" Arnie asks. (He's been unable to scrub the jiggly jingle from his head all these years, and sings it: "Rinso White, Rinso White, / Happy little washday song!") Pete smiles deprecatingly; for once he doesn't know, but fills us in about his rare, square, white house, built of steel panels in 1937 to a design credited to William Van Alen, architect of the Chrysler building in Manhattan. (That landmark's signature tower is not quite visible from Spanakos's deck, though on a clear day the Empire State building is—and the Twin Towers were.) The house is known in the neighborhood as "the sugar cube."

Two houses over on Ocean View Avenue, new owners have expanded and completely redone my friend Harvey Weiss's place, closing a secret cave used by Harvey's father in rum-running days during Prohibition. They've also done away with a little fountain and mini-pool in which Harvey and I, sometimes with his German shepherd, Trooper, used to fool around. Also gone is the wooded stretch that I cut through in the '40s, coming from my attached brick house on Surf Avenue. Now there are a couple of bumptious homes.

To the right through the Spanakos' dining room window, a scattering of blackened stumps is all that remains of the Atlantic Yacht Club and the pier from which steamers sailed daily to and from Manhattan's Battery Park, forty minutes (and forty cents) each way. Ted Arenson lived nearby on Maple Avenue in a house almost identical to mine; he took the ferry a few times with his father, who worked off Wall Street. A bunch of us used to play softball on what was left of the yacht club's parking lot, where Morgans, Whitneys and other fat cats rolled up in their limos before World War I, but houses have taken over there, too. Pete notes that two newer Ocean View Avenue neighbors are Mordechai Ben-David, world-famous Hassidic singer, and Dr. June Reinisch, an artist, house designer, collector extraordinaire and bio-psychologist who directed the Kinsey Research Institute.

(Her husband, Dr. Leonard Rosenblum, reportedly runs the biggest primate lab in the United States at Downstate Medical Center in Brooklyn.)

A cartoon not long ago in *The New Yorker* gives an exotic view of Sea Gate, wherein a 9-year-old fantasizing about neighborhoods in Brooklyn summons up Sea Gate, "with its maze of Venetian canals, from which, once you entered, you'd never emerge." O land of myth and mystery! Of fable and foolery! My once and former home town! The community that Nobel Prize author, Isaac Bashevis Singer, who fetched up in the Gate in 1935, called a paradise—next to the hell of Coney Island.

In the Morgan-Whitney-Dodge-Vanderbilt era, says Spanakos, a sign on the grass in front of the chapel, just inside the main gate on Surf Avenue, read, No Dogs or Jews. By the Depression, the tables were turned. When Arnie, Ted and I grew up, Sea Gate was all but middle-class Jewish—and there were plenty of dogs. Today, non-Jews make up an estimated fifteen percent of the 6,000-plus residents. Take Spanakos, and presumably Mel Salamone and Roseann Savasta, moved from an apartment across Gravesend Bay for room to keep the stray dogs they adopt (up to twenty by one recent report).

Now it's time to pass the ball to fellow former Gater Arnie "Wah Wah" Rosen, whose nickname tracks to teenage basketball days in our so-called Riviera, by Beach One. Arnie had the same kind of tenacity as his hoopster namesake, the redoubtable Wah Wah Jones of the University of Kentucky. Evidently this trait later helped Arnie to write and have published more than twenty books on office technology and computer systems. Now he's done a lot of legwork in searching out former Gaters. Enjoy the book!

Eli Flam

CHAPTER 1

HISTORY

We shall not cease from exploration
and the end of all our exploring
will be to arrive where we started
and know the place for the first time.

—T.S. Eliot

In the Indian summer of 1609, Henry Hudson reportedly anchored off what is today Sea Gate, the western tip of Coney Island. Like many explorers before him, Hudson, an Englishman whose voyage was financed by Dutch businessmen, was searching for a northwest passage to Asia. On September 2, his sailing vessel, the *Half Moon*, was anchored in what is now Lower New York Bay.

"Far to the northward of us we saw high hills," Hudson's mate, Robert Juet, wrote in his journal. "This is very good land to fall in with, and a pleasant land to see."

On September 3, Juet wrote, "The morning misty until ten o'clock, then it cleared, and the wind came to the south-south-east, so we weighed, and stood to the northward. The land is very pleasant and high, and bold to fall withal." In what they called a harbor—

now the deep crescent of Gravesend Bay—crewmen cast about constantly to mark the depth. Others rowed ashore to fish with the ship's net and caught "ten great mullets, of a foot and a half long a piece and a ray as great as four men could haul into the ship." The next night, "the wind blew hard at the north-west, and our anchor came home, and we drove on shore, but took no hurt, thanked be God, for the ground is soft sand and ooze."

"This day the people of the country came abroad of us, seeming very glad of our coming, and brought green tobacco, and gave us of it for knives and beads. They go in deerskins loose, well dressed. They have great store of maize or Indian wheat, whereof they made good bread. The country is full of great and tall oaks."

Indians were no strangers to Hudson and his crew. Earlier, after crossing the Atlantic, they had headed south to the coast of Virginia, where the English had landed two years earlier and set up a colony at Jamestown. Now, wrote Juet of the Sea Gate-to-be, "Our men went on land there, and saw great store of men, women and children," apparently from the Canarsie tribe. Further, woods abounded with "a great store of very goodly oaks." An Indian gave Juet dried currants, "which were sweet and good."

He also reported: "This day many of the people came aboard, some in mantles of feathers, and some in skins of divers sorts of good furs. Some women also came to us with hemp. They had red copper tobacco pipes, and others things of copper they did wear about their necks. At night they went on land again, so we rode very quiet, but durst not trust them."

On September 6, Hudson sent crewmen to further sound the depths, and en route they found land "as pleasant with grass and flowers, and goodly trees, as ever they had seen, and very sweet smells came from them." As they were returning, though, with no explanation given by Juet, a fight ensued with two dozen Indians from a pair of canoes. An Englishman, John Coleman, was slain by an arrow through his throat, and two others wounded.

Soon the ship sailed northward. On a broad river—later named for the Hudson but some hundred and fifty miles, the bottom became too shallow for the *Half Moon*, and the ship turned back.

By 1654, Coney Island—named most likely by the Dutch for the abundant *konijnen*, or rabbits, that ran wild through sand dunes and scrub grass—was acquired from the Indians by the town of Gravesend, on the north arc of the bay, and a shell road was built to join the two communities.

Coney Island developed a reputation for fast living, or at least danger-fraught fun; its western tip was a redoubt for adventurers from early days, while John "Chief" McKane, operating at the heart of Coney, was sent to Sing Sing Prison for rigging an election in 1892. (See the timeline below for details.)

By the turn of the twentieth century, tone and substance had done an about-face. The likes of the Morgan, Dodge and Vanderbilt families were instrumental in founding the Sea Gate Association. With a fence twelve feet high to keep out undesirables, instead of Denis Hamill's "epicenter of world depravity," the Gate entered the new millennium as a den of decorum. Maybe the high-living Stanford White, for one, soon to be killed by Harry K. Thaw over the affections of a showgirl, carried on in the vicinity of his Atlantic Yacht Club on Gravesend Bay, but no such record comes to hand. Still on the horizon were Noble Prize-winning author Isaac Bashevis Singer and the redoubtable Dr. Martin Couney, inventor of the infant incubator plus a mix of souls who made the Gate, in an earlier epoch, per the *New York Daily News*, "a center of corruption, communism and controversy." Whatever hyperbole has surfaced about the community, the question remains: Which does the vaunted fence do more of, keeping outsiders out or insiders in?

A TIMELINE OF HISTORIC EVENTS

In 1609, Captain Henry Hudson and the crew of the *Half Moon* explored Sea Gate/Coney Island, the first time Europeans set foot on the area.

In 1643, Lady Moody, an English noblewoman, emigrated from England. She sailed with a small band of followers that sought a religious haven for her Anabaptist beliefs. She arrived in the Dutch province of New Amsterdam. Governor Willem Kieft granted the group refuge and issued a charter for the establishment of a town from which she devised a master plan, the first of its kind in the New World. The grant comprised what would today be Sea Gate, Coney Island, Brighton Beach, Homecrest, Manhattan Beach, and Sheepshead Bay.

In the 1800s, Coney Island became a locale for investment, exploitation and enjoyment for many people.

In 1840, Mike Norton, a politician described as corrupt and nicknamed "Thunderbolt," opened Norton and Murray's Pavilion at Norton's Point, where Sea Gate lies today. Most of the surrounding land remained undeveloped for many years.

In 1871, William Macy "Boss" Tweed, leader of Tammany Hall, hid out in Sea Gate after escaping from prison in Manhattan.

In 1888, William K. Ziegler, president of the Royal Baking Powder Company, and Aldrick Man, president of the Sea Beach Railroad, proposed a plan to develop Sea Gate as an upper-class neighborhood.

In 1892, the Norton's Point Land Company purchased all the land west of West Thirty-seventh Street in Coney Island, bounded by the Atlantic Ocean on the south side and Gravesend Bay on the north side of this triangular peninsula. They named this newly acquired land, Sea Gate. The wild and barren tract of land, considered by some the most beautiful waterfront for hundreds of miles along the Atlantic coast, was soon leveled, streets were opened, and sewers laid. Redbrick sidewalks were set; many still exist today. Trees, mostly silver poplars, were planted.

During the next seven years, the Norton's Point Land Company sold many homes. It was emerging as a place of great houses and summer people; and had a year-round population of three thousand.

In 1899, a large number of local people, who already owned land or houses—including the Morgan, Dodge, and Vanderbilt families—bought the Norton's Point Land Company's holdings.

On July 15, a certificate of incorporation was issued by the state of New York for the formation of a private corporation known as the Sea Gate Association. The association and its members retained control of future development and installed gates at Surf and Mermaid Avenues and a fence twelve feet high to keep out visitors from Coney Island.

In the late 1890s, the Atlantic Yacht Club opened. Governor Al Smith of New York stayed at the club regularly from 1920 to 1928; British yachtsman Sir Thomas Lipton was one of many visitors.

In 1900 the famous architect, Stanford White inspired the building of the chapel, several slumber homes for the members of the Sea Gate Association. It was at this time that David Sarnoff, of RCA, operated a wireless station in Sea Gate, which borders on West Thirty-seventh Street and Surf Avenue.

AT THE TURN OF A CENTURY

The Sea Gate Association: Setting Policies and Codes of Behavior

The Sea Gate Association was composed of a board of directors and four committees—finance, grounds, transportation, and legal. Situated on the lower reaches of New York Harbor, Sea Gate was created as a community within the limits of the city of New York with private streets, and its own governing board, police and sanitation services. The expenses of maintaining, lighting and cleaning the streets, plus policing the grounds and beaches, providing lifeguards and operating a private boat service, were met with dues of the members based on the assessed value of their property.

The association further stipulated in its bylaws that residents maintain their lawns, flower gardens, and trees. Homeowners could contact the association office if they needed handymen at a price to cut grass, wash windows, beat rugs, and perform other chores.

Utilities

Built at a cost of $300,000 (in 1900 dollars) were underground cables, the sewage system, together with water and gas mains and electric light service, to serve 25,000 feet of streets, curbs, and sidewalks.

Traffic and Transportation: Autos

Entering 1900, paving of roads and streets was necessary to meet the needs of newly licensed Sea Gate drivers. Although autos were very rare, these new roads allowed residents convenient access to driving through Brooklyn's emerging systems of roads and parkways.

As owners of autos increased, the association mandated that drivers (*a*) must not exceed 15 miles per hour within Sea Gate, (*b*) mufflers must be kept silenced, and (*c*) lamps on autos must be lighted at night. Chauffeurs who violated these rules were not to be allowed back into Sea Gate.

The contents of a letter to the residents of Sea Gate from the Association in 1923 cautions drivers about speeding:

To the residents of Sea Gate:

The speeding of motorcars is dangerous to those who live here and is destructive to the roads.

The license numbers of speeding cars will be taken and after a warning, the second offence will cause the car to be excluded from Sea Gate.

Speeding must stop.

All residents are requested to drive with care and consideration for others.

Very truly yours,

J. W. Tumbridge,
President

Trolleys

The Norton's Point trolley operated on a private right of way from Stillwell Avenue to West Thirty-seventh Street. Many parts of the ROW are still visible today. Photo courtesy of Robert Presbrey

Trolleys which clang-clanged throughout Brooklyn for most of the first half of the twentieth century, soon became a main mode of public transportation for Sea Gaters. They had their choice of two east-west trolley routes. One ran along Surf Avenue from West Thirty-seventh Street east until it joined up with Gravesend (McDonald) Avenue.

The second shorter route was known as the Norton's Point Line. It started at the Gate and traveled on a right-of-way between Surf and Mermaid avenues and climbed up an incline to the elevated Stillwell Avenue subway station in Coney Island.

Arnold Rosen (left), Don Robins (right). Photo taken at 3780 Surf Avenue, Sea Gate, circa 1935. Note Norton's Point trolley across the street.

Trolleys were parked inside Sea Gate across the street from my home at 3780 Surf Avenue.

The transit company hired a watchman/cleaner named Tony. When he wasn't around, some of us kids would enter the stilled trolleys and by moving the lever on the controller pretend to be the motorman steering the cars through the streets of Coney Island. Benign mischief in our youth in the 1930s and '40s.

Interior of trolley (left) Trolleys parked on side of tennis court field (right). Photos courtesy of Robert Presbrey.

The seats were made of wooden slats and the backs had handles so that patrons could reverse them in the direction they were traveling. The overhead panels inside the cars were lined with poster ads for the likes of Bon Ami cleaner, Pepsodent toothpaste, U.S. War Bonds, civil service tutoring to become a police officer by the Delehanty Institute and Lucky Strike cigarettes. The interior of the cars was mostly kept clean and the outside was graffiti free. The Norton's Point Trolley ended service in December 1948 when the line was converted to motor bus operation on the streets.

My memories of playing in the empty trolleys were tame, however, compared to an incident described by Lenny Wachs with some friends who actually engaged the motor and drove the trolley within Sea Gate.

The Norton's Point trolleys were parked on Surf Avenue alongside the tennis courts. We used one of the empty trolley cars as a clubhouse. One day we decided to try to take the trolley for a ride. We thought we knew how to start the trolley and manipulate the controller since we rode the trolley to Stillwell Avenue with our parents dozens of times and watched the motorman. We connected the pole to the overhead line and the electrical connection was made. The motorman usually carried a key, which we didn't have. I seem to remember one of my friends had a pair of pliers and manipulated the switch, engaged the brake handle and the trolley started to move along the tracks toward the bay. A Sea Gate motorist crossed the tracks and we collided with him.

The Sea Gate Police arrived on the scene and Officer Sam Past called the transit authority and the Sixtieth Precinct police and drove us back to the police station. Although the motorist was unharmed he filed a suit against us. The case was dismissed because the judge determined that the transit company did not take adequate security measures to prevent unauthorized access to the trolleys.

Lenny Wachs

As a youngster, I tossed rocks at the trolley that used to bisect Sea Gate. I missed and broke a window. The conductor came right to our house on Surf Avenue. We hid under the bed on the second floor but my mother dragged us out to "face the music."

Joel Harnett

Tracks of the Norton's Point trolley run through the front lawn of the Ocean Breeze Hotel (at right). Photo by Robert Presbrey

I remember riding the Norton's Point trolley line through the narrow passageway between Surf and Mermaid Avenues. The trolley would make stops every two blocks to discharge and take on passengers. During the summers we would ride with the windows open and take in the sounds, sights and smells of Coney Island. As we got off at the Stillwell Avenue station, I could smell the mix of motor oil, lubricants and hear the screeching sound of the subway cars pulling out of the station, heading north to the rest of Brooklyn and to Manhattan. Spread out below, toward the boardwalk, were the attractions of "the Island." As I walked into the big terminal I could smell salt water taffy, cracker jack candy, hotdogs, French fries, and roasted peanuts and hear the sounds of newspaper salesmen hawking the Daily News *and* Daily Mirror; *the pitchmen barking at the people, "Hit the milk bottles and win a doll, only a nickel;" and in the distance, the clank-clank of the Cyclone sounded as the cars climbed up the track and then, the screams of the riders as the coaster plunged downhill.*

Harold Rosen

Boats and Water Transportation

Private steamboat service from Liberty Island Pier in the battery section of lower Manhattan to Sea Gate began in the last decade of the nineteenth century. Private boat service by the steamboats *William Coleman* and the *H.A. Haber* took forty-five minutes and ran everyday except Sunday. On May 21, 1917, the steamboat *Sea Gate* took over the route, with a fare of forty cents for single trips and $6 for a book of twenty. Below are two actual schedules.

Private Steamboat Service from New York to Sea Gate

In effect from May 21 to October 22, 1900, between Liberty Island Pier, Battery and Sea Gate

LEAVE SEA GATE	LEAVE NEW YORK
7:00 A.M.	8:00 A.M
8:00 A.M.	12:30 P.M
9:00 A.M.	1:30 P.M
2:15 P.M.	3:30 P.M
3:00 P.M.	4:15 P.M
4:30 P.M.	5:30 P.M

Private Steamboat Service

Commencing Monday, May 21, 1917, the steamboat *Sea Gate* will run between New York and Sea Gate everyday except Sundays to and including October 18, 1917, upon the following schedule:

LEAVE SEA GATE FOR NEW YORK	LEAVE BATTERY PIER FOR SEA GATE
8:00 A.M.	9:00 A.M
10:00 A.M.	1:30 P.M
2:15 P.M.	3:30 P.M
4:15 P.M.	5:30 P.M

My father worked in the city. He took the subway in the morning, but enjoyed taking the ferry back home to Sea Gate. I remember during the summer months, walking with my mother to the pier to meet the ferry that took my father home from downtown New York. We all walked home together and he would change into his bathing suit and we went for a swim in the lagoon that formed at Beach Forty-fourth Street.
Evalyn Greenstein-Krown

One summer I worked on Wall Street. I commuted by ferry, which docked a few blocks away from my office. It was perfect. I had coffee, soda, snacks on board and it sure beat the non-air-conditioned subways. There were

mornings when I left my house running on the sand, shoes in hand calling "Wait for me!" The captain was great. He waited for me every day.

Arlene Bergen-Greenfield

Rotting carcass of ship, "SYLTH" that carried passengers from Sea Gate to the Battery. Photo by Phil Horn, circa 1950

I recall my father commuting to work everyday aboard the Mayflower *and later the* Sylph. *Both boats took Sea Gaters to work from the Sea Gate pier to the battery in Manhattan.*

Leonard Everett Fisher

I still remember exploring the remains of an ancient wooden excursion/ferry boat from Manhattan on the beach at Beach Fifty-first Street where I would launch my twelve-foot gaff-rigged wooden sailboat made in Yugoslavia, to sail the lower bay.

Bob Tannen

The Beach

Of all the amenities Sea Gate had to offer its residents, the wonderful beach was perhaps the crown jewel. In the 1900s this strand was a broad, gently sloping stretch of hard, clean, fine white sand, which extended for approximately a quarter of a mile from West Thirty-seventh Street on the east to Beach Forty-sixth Street on the west and varied in width from one hundred to three hundred feet. It commanded the ocean view to the east, south, and west.

Bulkheads were constructed all along the waterfront and a fence, known as the Gate, was erected along the shoreline. The surf bathing was excellent.

A bathing pavilion was constructed for Sea Gaters and their guests. This building provided large, commodious rooms, with shower baths in both the ladies' and men's "apartments"[2] and the "roof garden," with its large lounges and easy chairs, was a favored spot for pavilion members. Regulations for beach members included: (1) Tents could not be erected on the beach against the bulkheads without the approval of the superintendent, (2) Ball playing was not allowed on the space known as the bathing beach and batting of balls was not allowed on any part of the beach, (3) Dogs were not allowed on the beach. The notice went on to say, "If this rule was violated, the Board of Health and the Society for the Prevention of Cruelty to Animals [ASPCA] will take charge of this matter, and hereafter will send the dog catcher's wagon into Sea Gate each week to pick up all dogs found on the streets or the beach, without muzzles and leash and destroy them." This was a drastic and politically incorrect directive, even for 1917 standards. Imagine the protests of the PETA group today, if any community stipulated these conditions.

The Atlantic Yacht Club

Another of Sea Gate's premier amenities was the Atlantic Yacht Club. Located at the northern edge of the island on Poplar

Avenue, it was an imposing structure that was designed by Stanford White. The club reigned supreme as the center of social activities and parties from 1890 until 1934 when it burned down. The night of the fire, many of the residents of Sea Gate watched the flames envelope and level the once-grand, wooden structure. Some Sea Gaters went into the charred remains and confiscated relics for souvenirs. "My older brother salvaged a pair of ornate andirons [metallic stands used to hold wood burned in a fireplace]," recalled Noel Schwartz. They now stand near his fireplace, as a treasured keepsake, in his home in Neponsit, New York. Lou Powsner, Jerry Reichenthaler, Jerry Leibowitz and his friends played roller hockey on the floor of Yacht Club months after the fire. Oddly enough, the floor survived and part of the ceiling supported by pillars.

> *I was a big stamp collector in those days. Two weeks after the fire, I looked around the burned structure and came upon some office furniture and files. I found some stacks of letters and envelopes with stamps and the "Atlantic Yacht Club" logo and postmark. I still have these "treasures."*
> **Eddie Mann**

Regattas and yacht racing were big attractions at the club's pier. Competing well-heeled society yacht owners dropped anchor off the pier and entered races beginning in Sea Gate, down the Jersey coast to Atlantic City to the lighthouse at Cape May and back to Sea Gate. Races were held nearly every Saturday in season. Several members of the club donated sterling silver trophies— the work of the noted sculpture Theodore B. Starr—to regatta winners.

A keen yachtsman, Sir Thomas Lipton, who first challenged for the America's Cup in 1899 with his yacht, *Shamrock I,* regularly docked at the club when he visited Brooklyn. He made five attempts to win the cup, but never succeeded. However, he earned a reputation as "the world's best loser," and was presented with a gold cup by the people of America for his good sportsmanship. In 1899, in one of Lipton's bid for the America's Cup Race, Guglielmo Marconi, the inventor of wireless communication, was assigned to report the event on behalf of the *New York Herald*. Marconi anchored his ship, the SS *Ponce*, near Gravesend Bay and set up his apparatus on board.

The virtues of the AYC are described in the June 1917 issue of *The Sea Gate Bulletin*,[3] published by The Sea Gate Association.

> *One of Sea Gate's chief attractions is the Atlantic Yacht Club. There is no yacht or country club in the vicinity of New York, which is so accessible. Instead of using the subway, a person doing business in lower New York has but a short walk to the Statue of Liberty dock, which is followed by a forty-five-minute trip on a well-run, comfortable and exclusive boat which makes the most humid summer day not only bearing, but alluring.*
>
> *The Club House is an imposing structure of which Sea Gate may be well proud. It is roomy, well ventilated and splendidly equipped. Its spacious verandas in the hottest weather are as cool as the deck of an ocean liner. They command a fine view of the exquisite sunsets which may be seen to better advantage there than elsewhere in this vicinity.*
>
> *Members and their wives may live at the Club House the whole season through if they so desire. The rooms used by bachelors both in the Club House and in the Annex are spacious, commanding a fine view of Gravesend Bay and the lower harbor. Bathers may don their bathing suits in their own rooms, thereby avoiding the nuisance of the stifling bathhouses found in most resorts. Every facility exists for first-class yachting, rowing, tennis, and billiards.*
>
> *The Pandemonium, erected in 1912, is a*

dancing pavilion without equal. Its dimensions are large. It has a perfect floor and owing to its open sides it is cool on the warmest nights. The splendid orchestra is well known. During the season dances take place on Wednesday and Saturday nights.

Everything possible is done to make the Club attractive to members and their guests. Members wives and daughters may be registered for the season and have access to the Club House and tennis courts.

The rule prohibiting non-members residing in Sea Gate from using the Club House and grounds will be strictly enforced. Initiation fees and dues are most reasonable. Junior members who must be between the ages of 18 and 22, are required to pay but one-half of the dues and no initiation fee. The cuisine is most excellent and seafood is a specialty. The Club opens officially May 30th.

The Atlantic Yacht Club was the second largest of its kind in the country and the only one at the time that had its home on the waters of New York Harbor.

An article in *The New York Times* of August 14, 1898,[4] describes the virtues of Sea Gate:

As a prophet is not without honor save in his own country, it is safe to assume that there are many New Yorkers who know Sea Gate only from the decks of steamboats or ocean steamers as they pass it on their way to and from Sandy Hook or Europe. To these unfortunates Sea Gate calls—and let them heed her call. The cognoscenti, and they are growing to be many in number, have paraphrased the old saying of "See Naples and die" into "See Sea Gate and survive," and after a visit there on one of these steaming summer days, when New York becomes a Turkish bath, one feels when the cool ocean breeze blows over Sea Gate

*sands, bringing life and health and vigor, that it pays
to be one of the cognoscenti.*

> *"Good bye to pain and care;*
> *I take mine ease to-day.*
> *Here, where these sunny waters break.*
> *And ripples this keen breeze—I shake*
> *All burdens from the heart,*
> *All weary thoughts away."*

Early Historical Sites

In addition to the Atlantic Yacht Club, the Sea Gate Chapel,
located at 3700 Surf Avenue, was built around 1900. It was
inspired by Stanford White and designed by the prominent
Brooklyn architectural firm of Parfitt Brothers. Services were non-
sectarian and the expenses to maintain the chapel were paid entirely
out of voluntary contributions. In addition to religious services,
the chapel was used for meetings, fund-raising activities and special
events. During World War I, the Sea Gate Auxiliary of the
American Red Cross met there to make surgical dressings for the
United States Military Relief. The chapel continues to serve the
neighborhood as a community center.

Most Sea Gaters shopped outside the Gate for groceries,
hardware and supplies. One of the first commercial vendors inside
the Gate was Sam Simon, who operated the Sea Gate Market,
by the Mermaid Avenue Gate, and sold a variety of meats and
chicken.

In the early 1910s the tennis court was laid between Mermaid
and Surf Avenues. Noteworthy homes continued to spring up,
most of them surrounded by landscaped gardens.

In 1908 the facing on the main Surf Avenue gatehouse was
reshingled and an executive office was built where the clerk of
the association and trustees met regularly. The Sea Gate Grounds
Department performed maintenance on the fence along Thirty-
seventh Street. Because of drifting sand, the fence was nearly buried

on the northern end and was raised by splicing posts to the old fence and using a fine wire mesh fence, instead of pickets.

A vacant plot of land at the foot of Beach Fiftieth Street, at the far end of the Gate, was designated as a park in honor of Charles A.

. A dedication ceremony took place on July 4, 1928. Mayor Jimmy Walker and Governor Alfred E. Smith, along with representatives of the aviation corps, army and navy, were present. A special children's parade was included in the ceremony. The park was renamed after World War II in honor of war hero Collin Kelly, but it is still referred to as Lindy Park.

CHAPTER 2

AN EARLY GATED COMMUNITY

Safety and Security or a Walled Enclave?

> *The same winds that sweep over Coney Island sweep also over Gate to the Sea. The same sand that sifts along Coney's Atlantic shore is the same sand that sifts along Gate to the Sea's Atlantic shore. And it's the same ocean, Mother Atlantic, who knows no bounds, who dances and plays along whatsoever land she pleases. The same sand, same winds, same ocean, same land. But Coney and Gate to the Sea are not the same. A barrier stands between the two. A wall in some places, a fence in others, trimmed all along with barbed wire. Barbed wire tears and stings. It cuts the flesh and makes it bleed. Though Coney and Gate to the Sea are made of the same stuff, a wall of blood separates them[5].*

The passage above may be full-blown hyperbole but it shows the kind of reaction that fences, walls and their ilk can summon.

Sea Gate was not the first gated community but it might be New York City's first. The Great Wall of China remains one of the great wonders of the world. Stretching four thousand five hundred miles, from the mountains of Korea to the Gobi Desert, it is more than two thousand years old and was built to protect an ancient Chinese empire from marauding tribes from the north. The earliest gated communities were built in England in the middle of the first century by the occupying Romans. In A.D. 122 the Emperor Hadrian ordered the building of a wall across the country from the Tyne to the Solway to separate the land of the Britons from the land of the Picts. When it was built in stone, the wall was some seventy-three miles long and five meters high. It was one of the Roman Empire's greatest feats of engineering.

Gated and walled military communities were established in the New World, in Spanish fort towns in the Caribbean. The first purely residential gated neighborhoods appeared in the U.S. in the late 1800s. Wealthy citizens of St. Louis and Tuxedo Park in New York built gated communities for protection from intruders and troublesome aspects of a rapidly developing urban society. When the Sea Gate Association was founded in 1899, one of its very first acts was to erect gates at the two entry points of Surf and Mermaid Avenues and install a twelve-foot fence the length of the Thirty-seventh Street strip that separated Sea Gate from Coney Island.

Other Gated Communities

Private communities now are popular in many areas of the nation, usually for the well-to-do and the very rich and often built around a lake or a golf course. Many ex-Sea Gaters have retired to Sunbelt states like Florida and Arizona. What is different now is that a growing portion of middle-class families (where the breadwinner is still working) has chosen to wall themselves off, opting for limited private government, and police. From Klahanie in Bear Creek, Washington to Oakwell Farms in San

Antonio, Texas; the Mai Kai Condos in Orlando; or the Doubletree Ranch Road complex in Scottsdale, Arizona, private communities are flourishing. Typically these residential retreats are private, gated, and governed by a thicket of covenants, codes, and restrictions. Setha Low states in her book, *Behind the Gates* (Rouledge 2003) that in the last twenty years, thousands upon thousands of the upper and middle classes have retreated into gated communities. She estimated that in 2002 one in eight Americans will live in these exclusive enclaves, which add up to more than sixteen million people.

Trends: Advantages and Drawbacks

More people are gravitating to gated communities because of concerns about crime and economic and social change. Some urban planners fear these changes will result in a negative effect on the social fabric of America. "The worst scenario for America with this trend would be to have a nation of gated communities where each group chooses to live among people just like themselves and ignores everyone else," said Milenko Matanovic, director of the Pomegranate Center, a nonprofit group from Issaquah, Washington, that works to build community links among suburbs.

Today the new form of gated community found in suburbs throughout the country attempts to ensure homogeneous economic, ethnic, and racial profiles.

Bob Tannen reflects on Sea Gate and the new gated communities across the country:

> *Sea Gate and Coney Island are historically the proto-typical models for waterfront resort communities and theme parks of this nation. They should be national historic sites, though much has changed and been disturbed over time. The so-called new urbanism of Seaside, Florida, and other new resort developments is based on the nineteenth-century idea of pedestrian,*

*friendly and small planned communities as resorts or
second home places.*

*Sea Gate, with wooden shingled cottages,
pedestrian scale along the beach and previously
served by a trolley system in the yards of houses along
Surf Avenue, is a better model of the new urbanism
and Disney World and its residential community
celebration is old Coney Island and old Sea Gate
combined.*

Gated communities have the following advantages:

1. Gates and fences provide the perception of security, safety and privacy.
2. Adding an attractive automatic gate system may translate into exclusivity and therefore increased property values.
3. Gates are often considered a cheaper alternative to hiring and managing security guards.
4. Livability and neighborliness of gated communities restore a lost sense of community.
5. Gated communities often provide self-contained amenities such as pools, spas, lakes, golf courses, and theater.

Gated communities have the following drawbacks:

1. Gates may be a barrier or hindrance to emergency services like the police or fire departments.
2. Residents may resent prohibitions against flagpoles, visible clotheslines, satellite dishes, streetside parking, and unkempt landscaping.
3. Double taxes are usually imposed on residents of gated communities.
4. Gates and fencing are not one hundred percent effective in crime prevention. Keypad codes for security gates may get into the wrong hands; low-paid security guards may be candidates for bribery and corruption.

The Sea Gate "Gate"

The main gate at Sea Gate on Surf Avenue in 1936.
At the left Doris Schwartz is pushing a stroller
with her grandson, Morris Shorofsky

Inserting electronic cards

Sea Gate intended to keep "undesirables" out with physical
gates, barbed wire (from bay to ocean), and a private police force.

These measures were created at a time when a new wave of European immigrants and poor people were discovering Coney Island and the shorefront communities in south Brooklyn. However, a new influx of ethnic groups gravitated into Sea Gate brought about by a stock market crash, several wars, and economic cyclical changes. As the process continues to this day, the difference in makeup of insiders and outsiders becomes less and less.

Sea Gate offers a powerful lesson in the advantages of private versus public ownership. Separated from the public housing and betimes decaying streets of Surf Avenue by a fence, Sea Gate's eight hundred homes now can be reached all year round only through the main gate on Surf Avenue, operated by the private Sea Gate police staff. Visitors must show proper identification before admittance is permitted. Public phones are provided at the Surf Avenue gate, to verify admission of those who do not have valid admission cards. Sea Gate residents with "electronic cards" insert them into an electronic pad, which opens the gate automatically. Originally Sea Gate had three gates. At time of writing, the Mermaid Avenue gate was closed. The Surf Avenue gate is operated twenty-four hours a day, seven days a week. The Neptune Avenue gate is open five days a week during the winter months with extended hours during the summer. Commercial vehicles must enter and leave by Surf Avenue; visitors may leave by any gate. In addition to the Gate patrol, a police car is continually patrolling Sea Gate streets. The police handle disturbances, police complaints, check vacant houses, and patrol community facilities. Most police activities are routine since the incidence of crime in Sea Gate is insignificant.

Shifting Sands and a Fence Fiasco

At the north end of Sea Gate, overlooking Gravesend Bay, a 10-foot chain-link fence was erected in 1997 to close a gap that opened when ocean currents brought enough sand to permit outsiders ready access to the Gate. Residents on Bay View Avenue, just outside Sea Gate, began to use the Gate's sandy strip for sunbathing, picnicking and fishing. Gaters though, were alarmed, and the private police force issued summonses to those it considered trespassers. Then the newly erected fence infuriated the residents of Bay View Avenue; they claimed that the beach belonged to the city and should be open to the public at large. City officials responded by ruling that the fence would have to be taken down.

The president of the Sea Gate Association, refused to do so. The city dispatched bulldozers and police cars to tear the fence down in a lightning strike that thrilled the Bay View residents. The case went to court—eventually to the New York Supreme Court—and the Sea Gate Association won the case. The city had to erect a new ten-foot fence.

> *Growing up happily in Sea Gate indeed was a special experience. The Depression years had passed, the war was over and everyone wanted to enjoy his or her lives more. Some went off the college, others moved. In September 1951, my family moved to Flatbush. However, many of my friendships continued and the joys of living in a gated community have made an indelible impression on me.*
>
> *Rosalie and Sheldon Spodek, Marilyn and Norman Rudow, and my husband, Jack, and I presently live in a gated community, a recreational development called Hemlock Farms, in Lords Valley, Pennsylvania. How prophetic!*
>
> *Irma Freedman-Most*

CHAPTER 3

GROWING UP IN SEA GATE

A Special Time and a Special Place

In the late 1940s, Brooklyn was not just the most heavily populated borough of New York City; it was seventy-five square miles of contiguous neighborhoods, each one like a small hometown. Sea Gate was a community of middle and upper-class Jews at Brooklyn's southwestern tip. Parents were just as likely to read the *Jewish Daily Forward* as the *Daily News* or *The New York Times*. It was an era of many an Oldsmobile in the driveway, washers and dryers in the basement, and egg creams, mellow rolls, and Charlotte Russes in the luncheonettes that were ubiquitous along Mermaid Avenue.

Hanging Out

In Sea Gate, teens would mostly hang out at the Sweet Shop, the Riviera, or the Whittier Inn. For kicks we would memorize the Hit Parade and Dodger batting averages and debated which was better ice cream—Hershey, Sealtest, or Breyers. There was no television except a few scattered homes like Mickey Becker's or Billy Schindler's.

This was Brooklyn before urban blight, before the Dodgers moved to Los Angeles. It was also a time of unbridled optimism. We won the big war, stopped Tojo, Mussolini, and Hitler, and—finally—began to integrate the major leagues. Sea Gate, like so many of the neighborhoods of Brooklyn, was a place of hope and opportunities. There was a feeling that in America you could transform yourself. We were the children who carried the high projections of our parents. As senior year in Lincoln High School approached for my crowd, Sea Gate was a place to hang on to while looking forward to college admissions or a place to want out of—maybe even joining the army. Eventually the Dodgers left and so did most of the guys and gals from Sea Gate. Some changed their names, moved to California and/or made money in the entertainment industry. Marvin Minoff became a TV producer, and Robert Summer, a CEO at RCA Records. David Sidikman became a New York State Assemblyman, while medical and law schools became the path for upward mobility for so many: Donny Robins specialized in pulmonary medicine; Morty Blum, gastroenterology; Martin "Buddy" Rubel, psychiatry; and Richard "Ducky" Oberfield specialized in oncology at the Lahey Clinic in Burlington, Massachusetts. But wherever they went, whatever they became, they took a little of Brooklyn and a lot of Sea Gate with them.

(Left to right) Morty Blum, Donny Robins, Richie Oberfield on Surf Avenue in Sea Gate. Freeze frame photo from old 8 mm home movie, circa 1948

It seemed the banks owned every home in Sea Gate but no one had a sense of being poor. We were on the beach, playing sports, and developing a healthy respect for achievement. Many successful business people like the Rifkins in cable (made it in Denver), the Dwormans in real estate or my friend, Dave Saunder, noted Harvard historian and author. We listened to records together as youngsters. He was always brilliant and a fine athlete.

Joel Harnett

The Beach

The beach was wonderful both during the summer and all through the year. Occasionally, a tanker would be beached or a plane would make a forced landing there. Massive ocean waves were produced when large boats such as the Queen Mary, Queen Elizabeth *or military convoys were returning from Europe into New York Harbor. The lifeguards always warned us in advance. The waves were strangely calm when ships were going in the reverse direction, out to Europe, from the harbor.*

Richard Oberfield

To most outsiders, distant, sleepy Sea Gate—the "Gate" to insiders—was beyond the outer reaches of the real world. It was a Brigadoon—a magical place where people awoke from their gray winter slumber each year on or about Memorial Day to play and sunbathe on the wide, seductive beaches until Labor Day.[6]

Leonard Everett Fisher

The pleasures of the Sea Gate beach, with its broad, sloping stretch of hard, clean fine white sand, was briefly described in chapter 1. For over a hundred years families had enjoyed the cool breezes, splashing in the surf and the beautiful ocean view.

Beach admission cards and later, beach passes were needed to gain entry. Beach passes were issued to owners and renters of property. Each person had to sign up at the Sea Gate Association's office, near the gate and then cross the street to the chapel to have your photo taken. I remember that Al Goldstein was in charge of photo taking in the 1940s. On summer weekends the beach became a meeting ground for teens, especially in the late 1930s and '40s. Blankets were spread and sun tan lotion applied as friends gathered for an afternoon of sunning, bathing, ball playing and socializing, including a lot of horsing around. Beach One, closest to the Surf Avenue gate, became the favorite because of its proximity to the Riviera restaurant and adjacent basketball and handball courts.

> In the summers I'd go down to the beach every morning, drop my towel in the sand and swim all day long. The kids on the beach would yell at me, "Come back, the water is too deep!" but I was a good swimmer and I'd swim up and back again from Beach Four to Beach One.
>
> It must have run in the family. My grandmother, Lena Simon, was a "Polar Bear." She swam in the ocean in Sea Gate and Coney Island all year long. I remember standing on the beach with chunks of ice floating all around her. She belonged to Bush Baths on the Boardwalk and would sunbathe in the solarium there and was brown from her head to her toes all the time.
>
> **Lenore Boni-DePillo**

> Each summer, as school was out, most days were spent at the beach, swimming and sunning to the strains of popular songs from the Riviera jukebox or a baseball game from someone's portable radio. We rode the waves to shore on our stomachs, held on to the ropes where the water was too deep to stand, practiced surface dives aiming to touch bottom and see how far

we could swim underwater, and built drippy castles or dug to China in the sand.

In time, perched on our blankets, we read long Russian novels or walked together or with a boyfriend from Beach One to Beach Four and back along the water's edge. Summer nights provided a background of special effects for everyone—the sounds of the sea— especially those nights when Sea Gate was enveloped in fog and we could hear the bell buoys and foghorns in the distance.

Florence Needle-Weingram

My first real boyfriend was Sandy Levine. He was a good-looking blond boy and an excellent athlete. Sandy had given me the little gold baseball and track letter that he received for being on varsity teams at Lincoln High. Sandy and I rarely went out alone. As was the style then, we traveled in groups that went to Luna Park or to the movies or to the Sweet Shop, a local hangout, or to somebody's house where we played records and danced.

In 1945, not long before I went on the Shubert tour, Sandy gave me a beautiful silver bracelet with the inscription, TO BUBBLES, THE STAR OF MY HEART. When I returned from the tour, I found out that Sandy had started dating a blues singer. I was a little surprised that our breakup didn't bother me at all, but I guess I shouldn't have been. I came back to Brooklyn a much worldlier young woman than when I'd left it.[7]

Beverly Sills

My family moved to Sea Gate in 1918. We lived at 3739 Oceanic Avenue. From Oceanic Avenue we had an unobstructed view of the ocean. Later, houses were built on Surf and Atlantic Avenues and we lost that wonderful view. Growing up I spent my summers on the beach. Most of the time I sat on the rocks and made

up stories about the seashell people imbedded in them.
Lucille Markow and Beatrice Nussbaum were my friends.
Theda Backalenick-Frank, Lincoln HS 1933,
Cornell 1937

During the summer weekends we would loll
on the beach during the days and plan house parties
in the evening. I would tell a few friends on the
beach we were planning a party that night and
twenty-five would show up. My dad would string
up colored lights in our garden on Laurel Avenue
and I would set up my 78 record player outside on
the porch and listen to the big bands. We were in
our late teens and early twenties and my Sea Gate
friends were Rhoda Krawitz, Rhoda Judd, Millie
Flam, Corrine Berg, and Sid Bucholtz (his father
had the butcher store on Mermaid Avenue). He
would always bring Norma Konigsburg. Sid and
Norma along with Sheldon Spodek and Rosalie
Firester were the first to marry in our crowd.
Arlene Bergen-Greenfield

The beach at night was magical. Our teen group
had beach parties and roasted "mickeys" in beach fires.
No permission was requested or needed and we never got
in trouble. We swam at night and I can still remember
the phosphorous jellyfish that lit up the black water as I
dove in. Beach Two was the ideal place. It had the best
jetty for diving. We caught crabs in the rocks that separated
Beach One and Two (the lagoon area).

I remember the horses that pulled the rakes to
clean the beaches every morning. I remember huddling
at the back of the beach at the end of the day to eat
half a sandy peanut butter and banana sandwich
left over from lunch.

I remember jumping from herringbone brick to
herringbone brick to find a "cool spot" as your feet

burned on the way to the beach. I remember swimming out to the bell buoy and those worms that fell from the trees into the spring puddles. I remember the games we played: Red Light, Green Light, jacks and marbles and Potsy and Ghost.

It was so comforting in Sea Gate to know someone on every street and having cousins and uncles and aunts and grandparents within walking distance. I remember George the cop at the Neptune Avenue gate, who filed Roman numerals into the cross bar of my bike to identify it in case it was stolen. I remember the Dugan man, the Brighton Laundry man, the fish man, the Good Humor man, and the milkman. I remember the trolley going all the way to the bay . . . And a million more memories of an enchanted childhood.

Diana Rubinstein-Wiener

At Beach One: front Row (L to R) Irma Goldman, Eileen ?, Sandy Levine; middle row (L to R) Sandy Levitt, Richie Ehrman; back row (L to R) Barbara Harnett, Gloria Harnick, Georgette Harnick

I recall the ship Leviathan *leaving New York in the dead of night to be scrapped in England. She was*

*all lit up with no passengers aboard. I stood in
Lindbergh Park with my father who was one of the
marine designers who converted the* Leviathan *into a
troop ship in 1917 after she was captured from the
Germans at her pier in New York. (She had been
known as* The Vaterland.*)*

Leonard Everett Fisher

**At Beach Four: Barbara Harnett and Irma
Goldman, circa 1942**

*My father used to read the shipping news section of
the paper and would tell me which ship would be arriving
or departing. We would go to the beach and look for the
ships and were able to identify each one by their silhouette
and smoke stacks. One smoke stack was OK, but if the
ship had two or three, that meant it would generate a
big wave and we had to get out of the water. When the*

*ship went around the bend at Gravesend Bay, it sailed
so close to us you felt as if you could reach out and touch
it. We recognized the* Bremen, *the* Isle de France, *the*
Normandie, *and the* Queen Mary.

Barbara Harnett-Weil

**At the Beach: Barbara Goldberg-Furman (left) and
Irma Freedman-Most (right) on Beach One, 1948**

**Young beachgoers. Don Robins always in the
company of a pretty girl. Circa 1933**

I recall sitting on Beach One, near the rocks, where Beverly Sills used to sit with her family. Theresa and Charlie Kalander lived next door to us on Lyme Avenue. Theresa's brother was George Burns, the comedian.

Harriet Harnett-Marks

Keeping a watchful Eye. Sea Gate Lifeguard Sandy Einhorn on Sea Gate Beach Three, circa. 1948

Sea Gate beach pass, Florence Needle, 1950

I hated the beach. I hated the sand. I hated the sun. My mother and father were great swimmers. My father was suntanned. He had olive skin. I was stark white. I was skinny and my parents were ashamed of the way I looked because people would remark to my parents: "What is wrong with her? She's so skinny! Don't you feed her? Why is she so green looking? You should get her a little color." Now a lot of my friends have some form of benign skin cancer and I have wonderful skin because I hid from the sun.

To get out of going to the beach, I had to be a little enterprising. When I was twelve years old, I started a day care service on my porch. I charged parents fifty cents or a dollar to watch their 4-5-and 6-year-old kids. We played games, did arts and crafts and that was my way of getting out of going to the beach.

Teri Seidman

I loved the beach during summer. I was a good swimmer and usually hung out at Beach One with Stanley Liebowitz, Eugene Goldberg, Dave Glickman, Jesse Wolfenson, Gil Christian and the Adler twins. I remember one day there was a run on whiting fish. The whiting were apparently being driven toward the shore and eaten by blues. The whiting tried in vain to escape and finally leaped on to shore by the droves. We would walk along the shore with baskets and picked up the whitings by the dozens.

Lenny Wachs

The Games We Played

Where did all those games go, the ones I threw myself headlong into as a boy, a rawboned kid who fell in love with the smell and shape of a basketball, who longed for its smooth skin on the nerve endings of my fingers and hands, who lived for the sound of its unmistakable heartbeat, its staccato rhythms, as

I bounced it along the pavement throughout the ten thousand days of my boyhood? The one skill I brought to the game was my ability to handle a basketball and if you tried to intercept me, if you moved without stealth or cunning, I would go past you. Even now that is a promise. I would pass you in a flash the entire game with you trying to catch me. I could move down the court with a basketball and I could do it fast.

Several times in my life I have gone crazy, and I could not even begin to tell you why. The sadness collapses me from the inside out, and I have to follow the thing through until it finishes with me. It never happened to me when I was playing basketball because basketball was the only thing that granted me a complete and sublime congruence and oneness with the world. I found a joy, unrecapturable beyond the realm of speech or language, and I lost myself in the pure, dazzling majesty of my sweet, swift game. [8]

Basketball at the Riviera. Freeze-frame photo from 8mm home movie, circa 1949. Marty Tankowitz, back to camera, Eli Flam, shooter, Mark Solomon, extreme right.

The Riviera was our Madison Square Garden and basketball

was our game. Most of us were good enough for pickup games but we didn't play on any high school teams. Eugene Goldberg was the exception.

He lived at 3920 Cypress Avenue and played varsity for Lincoln High School (class of June '47), but rarely played pickup games at the Riviera. Lincoln coach, Venty Leib, forbade varsity players to play schoolyard or pickup games.

Sea Gater, Eugene Goldberg (in dark uniform) goes up for a shot during Lincoln-Madison game on January 17, 1947. Lincoln won 43-41

We were all first-and second-generation Americans and parents mostly ruled. They instilled in us the value of education and made sure that schoolwork and studying came first. Most of our parents never attended college but they fully expected their sons and daughters to attend after graduation from Lincoln.

A shifting crowd played basketball at the Riviera; we played in the heat, in the cold, and sometimes in the snow, shoveling off the court—a converted pair of handball courts. On weekdays we would come home from Mark Twain Junior High or Lincoln, grab some milk and head for the courts. But it was the weekends that we lived for. We'd shed our overcoats in winter, tighten the laces on our Keds or Converse high-tops, choose up sides and play until our muscles ached and our legs couldn't move. At midday we would drag ourselves out the gate for a quart of milk and a Drake's Devil Dog at Gittler's grocery store and return to the Riviera for an afternoon session, then go home to listen to Marty Glickman announce the Knicks game at the Garden on WINS radio.

Eventually we formed a Sea Gate team. We registered for the *Mirror (New York Daily Mirror)* Parks Brooklyn Basketball Tournament and the Police Athletic League Basketball Tournament. We were a "rag tag" group but eventually coalesced into a harmonious team. Howie Fietel, a guard for the fabled Clair Bee at LIU (Long Island University), volunteered to coach us and we practiced in the evenings at the Mark Twain JHS Gym.

Freeze-frame photo from 8mm home movie. Howie Fietel (center in white shirt holding ball) during practice at Sea Gate Riviera courts. David Sidikman, (left of Fietel) now a NY State Assemblyman, appears in background, circa 1949.

We ordered our uniforms from Pat Auletta. He owned a sporting goods store across the street from Nathan's on Stillwell Avenue in Coney Island. The uniforms were satin maroon and gold with "Sea Gate" emblazoned on the jersey with a gold stripe embroidered on the shorts.

Pat was a sports enthusiast, active in the community, and an avuncular salesman for sporting goods. His store had lots of sporting pictures in the front window and walls. I bought my first and second baseball gloves, and set of spiked shoes from his store as well as baseballs and bats. He sold the ubiquitous pink Spaldeen rubber balls that had so many applications.

Sidney Krimsky

There was another Riviera game called box baseball. We drew a rectangular box on the handball wall for a strike zone. Two players would face each other. One batted, the other pitched. The batter, if he connected, would hit the ball past the pitcher for a single or over his head on a fly for a double, triple, or home run into designated zones into Beach One. We played with a pink rubber ball made by Spalding. The Spalding Sporting Goods Company manufacturered a pink rubber ball made from the rejected inner core of a tennis ball. The name "Spaldeen" (used in the remainder of the book) is a corruption of the pronunciation of "Spalding" by New Yorkers with thick accents. Our bats were sawed-off broomsticks.

Softball was played at the Sea Gate field (the old tennis courts).

Saul Weiser was the dominant softball pitcher. He had a blazing windmill-style, fastball. Freeze-frame photo from 8mm home movie, circa 1948

The returning World War II veterans formed teams within

"a league of their own." (An expanded discussion of softball appears in chapter 6, "The War Years.")

Football was also played at the tennis courts. Sea Gate had two teams, the Orioles and the Akers. They played each other and other neighborhood club teams. Eddie Mann, who played quarterback for Lincoln High School also played for the Akers. The team had uniforms but only had eleven helmets. When a substitute was brought in, the outgoing player would give the sub his helmet whether it fit him or not. Jerry Liebowitz, Jerry Reichenthaler, Lenny Mann and Cy Carr also played on the team. The team had winning records in 1934, 1935 and 1936. Championship games were played in the Parade Grounds and at Ebbets Field.

> *I used to play football at the tennis courts with my Akers teammates: Donald Steinberg and Harold Wagner. During Christmas week a tall fellow would hang around the tennis courts and watch us play from the sidelines. He always carried a whistle around his neck and would ask us if he could referee the game so he could blow his whistle. He assured us he knew the rules and would be observant and fair. We agreed to let him referee a few of our games. It turned out that he was a meticulous and conscientious referee and he added a professional touch to all our games. He would always return to the tennis courts to referee our games during his Christmas vacation from college.*
>
> *When he was away at college his mother would come into my store—Powsner's Men's Shop on Mermaid Avenue—and order shirts for her son. We became friendly and she would keep me apprised of her son Norman's career—a graduate of Alfred University, moved to Los Angeles, became a teacher, a principal and a football referee. I assumed she meant that he refereed high school games.*
>
> *One day in the fall of 1960 I was watching a*

Giant-Dodger football game when they announced the referee for the game. I was astonished to hear Norman's name as the senior referee. As the TV zoomed in on him, there was shy Norman wearing the traditional black-and-white zebra shirt as referee for a nationally televised NFL game. I continued to follow his career as a referee.

Years later I learned that Norman was to be the referee of the historic Giants-Philadelphia Eagles game at Yankee stadium on September 23, 1973. I asked his mother where he was staying and she gave me the name of his hotel. I called him at his hotel, reminded him that he used to referee our football games in Sea Gate and asked him if he had time for me to interview him for an article, ("From Sea Gate to the Super Bowl") I was going to write about him. He indicated to me that it would be impossible because he had scheduled meetings during the weekend. However, he suggested that I visit him outside the Yankee Stadium referee's dressing room before the game and that he may have a few minutes to talk with me. I met him there an hour before game time and he invited me to walk out onto the field as we talked. There we stood on the 50-yard line in the middle of a sold-out Yankee Stadium while footballs were flying overhead with the Eagles on one side and the Giants on the other side, taking their pre-game warm-ups. A spectacle I will never forget. He arranged for me to view the rest of the game in the Yankee Stadium press box. The game ended in a 23-23 tie and it was the last Giant football game to be played in Yankee Stadium.

Lou Powsner

The name of this tall, shy Sea Gate teenager who wanted to referee football games in the tennis courts was **Norman Schachter.** He was a senior referee for the NFL for twenty-one years and was the referee in Super Bowls I, V, and X. He also worked eleven championship games and refereed the first Monday Night Football Game. And as Paul Harvey would say, "Now you know the rest of the story."

Other Games

"**Territory**" was played with a penknife. We played across Surf Avenue at the end of the trolley tracks. To begin the game, we shaped out a border of the earth and divided it into various regions. We took turns by opening the blade and flinging it into the ground trying to connect into the largest portion of the earth.

> *We often played both stoopball on my steps and stickball with the gang on my street, Oceanic Avenue. Since the ball often would be hit on to the big, circular porch of the hotel, the owner was forever warning us he would call the police if we did not cease playing. We never did and he never stopped complaining.*
>
> *The large hotel, Max Gershunoff's Ocean Breeze Hotel, across the street was often used for the game of hide and seek in addition to playing football on the vast lawns during the winter when it was closed. It was great fun. We often had to be on the lookout for the caretaker who prohibited such activities.*
>
> *Richard Oberfield*

We had other benign games such as flipping baseball cards to nab the other guys, by matching yours or his face up. And when it rained, we took our games indoors when we were very young, and played with tinker toys, Erector Sets, Lincoln Logs, and Monopoly.

We could buy practically anything on the street just outside of the Gate, on Mermaid Avenue. (See chapter 5, "A Walk up Mermaid Avenue.")

Free time activities for a girl growing up in Sea Gate during the '40s and '50s were limited only by imagination. We roller-skated, jumped rope, played potsy and hopscotch and ball games like stoopball and handball—all with a pink Spaldeen, plus "A my name is Anna"(bouncing through the alphabet). We played in the snow and sledded down small hills on the empty lot between Oceanic and Nautilus Avenue before the "new houses" were built. We played with "cutouts" (paper dolls) and a Ouija board, played Monopoly and even mahjongg and made telephones and invisible ink.

Florence Needle-Weingram

I was a "Tom Boy," and liked to bike ride and play ball with the boys. Once I remember I got into a handball game at the courts on Beach One with this boy I didn't know. I won the game. The next day the kids told me I beat the best handball player in the Gate. (I still don't know his name.)

Lenore Boni-DiPillo

All my friends came home from PS 188 and changed their clothes. My mother didn't think I should change my clothes. I had to play in my dresses that my grandmother made. My grandmother made all my clothes. My teacher would send me from classroom to classroom so that all the other teachers could see the handmade dress that my grandmother made for me— little knitted dresses with intricate embroidery and pompoms. So I played in those dresses. My knees were scraped and my dress became soiled when I played emmies and potsy.

Teri Seidman

Our Schools

Nursery school for some Sea Gate children was their first experience away from parents. Parents had a few choices within Sea Gate—private or religious nursery schools. Congregation Kneses Israel had a yeshiva and offered half day programs for 3-year-olds through kindergarten age. They stressed Jewish history, values and pride. The children observed all Jewish holidays and celebrated Shabbat on Fridays with the rabbi. The classes were held in a connected annex to the main temple on Nautilus Avenue. I remember sitting in a classroom with a large map of Palestine and the Hebrew alphabet displayed in the front of the room. Gaverus Toy was my teacher and Mr. Leibik was my tutor who prepared me for my bar mitzvah. We attended Saturday services and bar mitzvah ceremonies and I was impressed with the stained glass windows, the ark and the regal aura of the temple itself.

A group of kids at Charlotte's Nursery on Surf Avenue (between Beach 38th and 40th Streets), circa 1935. Left to right: Harvey Glassman, Arnold Rosen and Donny Robins (at right in the white top and dark shorts). Charlotte is standing on the right.

There were also a few private nursery schools, usually housed in homes where rooms were designed to accommodate groups of eight to twelve children in a class. They provided safe and pleasant surroundings that prepared children for entry into primary schools. The Sea Gate Playland School was located on Beach Forty-seventh Street and provided transportation and lunches. Charlotte's Nursery was located on Surf Avenue and Beach Forty-second Street near an empty lot that was used for a playground, with swings and slides.

Charlotte's Sea Gate Nursery, circa 1936. Bottom Row: Donald Robins (4ᵗʰ from left); Ken Klein (6ᵗʰ from left) Middle Row: Len Friedman (2ⁿᵈ from left), Frieda Packrose (3ʳᵈ from left), Morton Gross (4ᵗʰ from left); Top Row: Arnold Rosen (1ˢᵗ from left), Alan Radetsky (3ʳᵈ from left), Malcolm Marquit (4ᵗʰ from left), Barton Meissner (5ᵗʰ from left), Merrill Hessel, (6ᵗʰ from Left), and Charlotte, Director of Nursery.

Our young Judea group, called "The Herzl Buds," met at the Center of Kneses Israel, where we debated issues and learned Israeli songs and dances. We formed our own informal Polly Pigtails Club. During the High Holy days, we dressed up in our new fall clothes and climbed the shul's wooden stairs to join our mothers in the women's balcony.

Florence Needle-Weingram

*I remember Camp AAA, Mrs. Magid's single
experiment running a day camp brought kids in from
all over Brooklyn. Francine Shorofsky (Silverblank),
Elaine Tarnapol, and I were hired as counselors.*
Irene Needle-Halpern

The nearest elementary school, three blocks outside the
Neptune Avenue gate, was PS 188.

PS 188

Some of our parents would drive us to school during our
kindergarten days but then we were allowed to walk on our own
in the early grades. I remember when it rained, my father would
put his overcoat over his pajamas and drive Donny Robins and
myself to school. Sometimes we walked home for lunch at noon
and walked back for the afternoon session and returned on foot

when classes ended at 3 P.M. In those days there were no talk of kidnappings or pedophiles lurking nearby and we were always careful crossing the streets along Mermaid Avenue. My route was usually the same. On my walk to school, I usually crossed the trolley tracks, cut through the tennis courts where I might be joined with some of my other Sea Gate friends. At Mermaid Avenue I would meet some of my classmates from Coney Island. Their apartments were clustered close to the school—from West Thirty-seventh to Twenty-eighth Street. We stayed friends throughout elementary school and into Mark Twain and Lincoln. After sixty years, their names evoke lasting friendships. Where have you gone, Marilyn Bernstein, Donald Springer, Howie Bean, Vivian Jablonick, Maxine Tannenbaum, and Robert Wind? A Coney Islander remembers Sea Gate and his friends:

> *Sea Gate and outside the Gate was all Jewish and white. The only African-American friend we had was Lou Gossett, the actor, who lived on West Thirty-fifth Street. The kids who lived outside the Gate thought everybody who lived in Sea Gate were rich. But we were all friends.*
>
> *My friends who lived in the Gate and who I went to school with were Eli Flam, Ted Arenson, Buddy Rubel, Harvey Weiss, Robert Summer, David Buxbaum and Monroe Korn. Some of the girls whose names I remember were Joan Brody and Evalyn Greenstein.*
>
> **Mort Weiner**

The school was a five story, redbrick structure that spanned a full block on Neptune Avenue between West Thirty-fifth and West Thirty-third Street. Monitors would have to take the chalkboard erasers to the roof and clean the erasers by banging them against the wall. The roof was enclosed in iron latticework and on nice days, we had gym classes up there. We walked to school, ate lunch that our parents prepared in brown paper bags, and we knew that our parents would "back up" our teachers no matter what the circumstances were. On assembly days we sang songs like "God Bless America," "Columbia, the Gem of the Ocean," and other patriotic songs. Sometimes one class performed a play or a talented student sang a song or played a solo musical number. During the holiday season we sang Christmas songs, even though most of the students were Jewish. No one seemed to mind, no one protested; the songs were beautiful and we all were in the holiday spirit.

In my day, PS 188 had classes from Kindergarten through the eighth grade. I graduated in 1934. I remember my English teacher, Mrs. Le Brun. She would ask, "Edwin, why aren't you as good as your father?"
Eddie Mann

When I went into kindergarten, my teacher, Mrs. Marder, couldn't understand why my father insisted that I only speak Yiddish. However, I learned English quickly. I brought lunch from home and ate with my friends in the lunchroom. I remembered the lunchroom always smelled of tomato soup.

My best friends were Betty Misrock, Rhoda Krawitz and Irene Neal—all from Sea Gate.
Martha Goldstein-Reinken

I entered PS 188 as a second grader. My class was a homogeneous group. My classmates, Barbara Goldberg and Barbara Leibowitz, became my first friends and we progressed together through PS 188 and Mark Twain JHS. During these years, several of our teachers were friends of our parents and neighbors—Yetta Kaplan, Fritzie Hessel, and Gloria Friedman.
Irma Freedman-Most

I was fortunate to be in the same class year after year with so many good friends: Eli Flam, Teddy Arenson, Buddy Rubel, Barbara Brill, Norma Diamond, Stanley

Felson, Merrill Hessel, Howard Esterces and Sheldon Burstein (Berman). Sheldon and I were in Germany in the U.S. Army at the same base for a while.

David Buxbaum

Bernie Kastenbaum and I had solos along with several others in the PS 188 Glee Club show of 1943. He was great but I got mike fright and flubbed my lyrics. In 1955 I was in the army in Germany and I talked with Bernie over the phone. He was stationed nearby in Karlsrue, Germany at the time.

Kalman Bergen

I remember elementary school at PS 188 and can still recall the names of my teachers in each grade. My classmates stayed together through all grades due to homogeneous grouping and this had the result of maintaining stability and long-term friendships. I recall the great parties after school in one or more homes and the games we played such as "spin the bottle," which led to future dating. I always liked the girls and had a girlfriend since the age of three. When girls and boys played like we were adults, I was always chosen to be the doctor.

Don Robins

Coney Islanders also shared their memories of PS 188 below:

I lived outside the Gate on West Thirty-third Street between Mermaid and Neptune Avenues, across from the schoolyard of P S 188. Most of the time we would play basketball, softball, touch football, punchball and stickball in the schoolyard.

Some of my teachers lived in Sea Gate. I particularly remember Mrs. Hessel (her son, Merrill was in my class) and Mrs. Stein (her husband, Dr. Stein, was a dentist who had an office on the corner of Mermaid Avenue and West Thirty-third Street). My friends and I would visit Dr. Stein to have dental notes completed which were required by the Board of Education at that time.

Mort Weiner

During the summer we would enter the building (we knew where the unlocked door was), climb the stairs to the top floor and watch the fireworks from the roof. I was always afraid of heights and would watch the fireworks on my knees, petrified if I looked down and fell on to the parapet or the street below.

Mickey Weinshanker

I actually entered first grade at Mark Twain Junior High School. In 1937-38 the Board of Education began an experimental (progressive) curriculum for first graders at Mark Twain. At the end of my third year, funding for the program ran out and the short-lived experiment ended. We all transferred to PS 188 and placed into the 4th grade. I was in the RA (Rapid Advance) classes at Mark Twain and I remember my Sea Gate classmates at the time were Ducky Oberfield, Morty and Joan Blum, Eddie Feinberg, Anita Orans, Burton Merriam and Robert Berkvist. I remember Robert as a tall, blonde that became a distinguished editor for The New York Times.

Donald Picker

Now it's the Michael E. Berdy School, and it has a program for gifted students, with admission by examination. Graduates of that program often move on to Mark Twain Junior High School, ten blocks from Sea Gate.

Mark Twan Junior High School

We walked to and from school, hauling our books, lunch, sneakers, and other stuff such as a baseball glove, Spauldeen and baseball cards for trading during lunch or recess. We had a "home room" teacher and changed classes every period, and were assigned different teachers for each class. White shirts and ties were required for the boys during assembly days and sneakers were banned (except for gym class). One of the biggest shocks I had was at the end of the first day, walking out of the door and down front steps and seeing the older girls smoking.

Perhaps for many of us, the "best years of our lives" were spent at Abraham Lincoln High School. We rode the bus from Sea Gate through Coney Island, and as we approached the elegant, tree-lined Ocean Parkway, Lincoln High was an imposing sight. Its manicured lawn, dotted with forsythia, rhododendron, and flowering cherry trees, swept toward the broad white building, bisected by a concrete walkway. To me, Lincoln resembled nothing so much as a Greek temple with a stone owl perched on the pediment. There were flagpoles on the front lawn and, near the front steps, an imposing statue of the Great Emancipator.

I was a cheerleader at Lincoln and Robert Summer, a fellow Sea Gater, was my partner. (I wonder if he could lift me today). We traveled with the basketball and football teams and had our time to cheer in Madison Square Garden.

Irma Freedman-Most

Lincoln High School Cheerleaders, 1951. Irma Freedman-Most and Robert Summer appear in second row from the top.

I met my husband, Eddie Gabay, when I was 14 and he was 17 in the cafeteria at Lincoln High School. He lived at 4401 Beach Forty-fourth Street and I lived at 3819 Cypress Avenue We dated all through

*high school but didn't marry each other until 18 years
later.*

Carole Mennen-Gabay

The memories of our high school days were of joys and regrets, triumphs and disappointments, but more often, an exhilaration of being part of a great high school. We kept busy with clubs, teams, and societies. In the late thirties, the Lincoln Log, the Art Gallery and the Lincoln Award were founded. And our athletic teams were competitive. By the end of the '30s, the enrollment zoomed from 3,000 to 8,150.

Sometimes a group of guys and gals would get together and meet in the cafeteria after the first period in the morning to play "hookey" for that day. It was usually on Fridays when the big movie houses in Manhattan changed their shows. One week we would see Jimmy Lunceford at the Loews State or Tommy Dorsey at the Roxy. I remember one morning there were five of us who walked out of the building (in those days there were no locked doors or security guards) and took the Brighton train to Manhattan to catch the movie and stage show at the Paramount. Jerry Reichenthaler, a Sea Gater who married a Barkin girl, was with us that day. The price for the early show at the Paramount was forty cents.

After the movie, the house lights came on, and the band would appear on the rising stage. Kay Kyser and his Kollege of Musical Knowledge *band performed. He appeared wearing a mortarboard and a black robe and the show also included vocalists* Ginny Simms, Harry Babbitt *and trumpeter* Merwyn Bogue, *"Ish Kabibble." The name* Ish Kabibble *was taken from an old Yiddish song titled* "Ish Ga Bibble" *and its loose translation is "I should worry?" After the show we went for lunch at*

*a Chinese restaurant, which cost us another forty
cents. What a wonderful day and glorious memories
of good times at Lincoln High.*

Lou Powsner.

In the '40s, the world was engulfed in a war and Lincoln rose
to the occasion. Pupils bought, equipped and sent an ambulance
to the war front. At one football game, war bonds totaling
$414,000 were sold. There were changes in the faculty, but the
dedication continued. In fifty years, Lincoln High School can be
justifiably proud to have contributed a Nobel Prize winner in
medicine and a Pulitzer Prize winner in drama. Lincoln alumni
have stood tall in the fields of sciences, theater, cinema, art, and
music.

*I graduated from Lincoln in June 1937, where I
was given a foothold on what was to be my life's work.
With the inspiration and guidance of Mr. Leon Friend,
who was head of the Graphic Arts Department, I
became a member, and later president of the art squad,
a student-run group that worked on school projects,
developed their portfolios, etc., and in a sense gave us
the very beginnings of a taste of what "commercial
art" was. I went right from high school into the field
and stayed in it until my retirement thirteen years
ago. I loved the work, and it was good to me and my
wife and four children.*

Bill Backalenick

Boy Scouts

*The Sea Gate Chapel stands out as the
headquarters of Boy Scout Troop 256. Here we met
every Friday night and enjoyed the camaraderie of
young boys and men working, learning, and playing
together. In World War II, the troop did our job*

collecting newspapers, tin cans, and other objects used in the war effort.

Don Robins

Tiger Patrol, Troop 256. Sea Gate Chapel, 1947. Bottom row (left to right): Donny Robins, Bernie Frank, Arnie Rosen. Top row (left to right): Dave Dolgenos, Sol Levy and Alan Sultan.

I was in the Sea Gate Cub Scouts. We met on Friday nights at PS 188. Most of the evening we played "Dodge Ball." The basement of PS 188 had pillars that we used to stand behind to shield us from the ball. Our den leader was Benjamin Salzhauer from Sea Gate and my fellow den members were Ronnie Teller, Ronnie Berliner, and Alan Altman. After the meeting we walked along Neptune Avenue and stopped into Stollers (between Thirty-sixth and Thirty-seventh Street). I remember it was in 1940, before the war and he charged us fifteen cents for an ice cream sundae.

Mel (Sonny) Krown

I was a member of Sea Gate's Troop 256. We met every Friday night in the Chapel—the big old wooden building across from the main gate. I was a patrol leader and Don Brenner, David Dolgenos, Frank Williams, Mort Blum, and Don Robins were also members. We went on overnight hikes and it was my job to convince the mothers that their thirteen-and fourteen-year-old boys would not get hurt or lost in the wilds of Spruce Pond (near the Red Apple Rest) near Suffern, New York. Our Scoutmaster was O. J. Alpert, and Stanley Ferber and Jesse Wolfenson were assistants. When we returned home from our weekend hikes we were greeted like long-lost explorers from the North Pole by the fearful parents.

Walter Spodek

Ready to go on an overnight Boy Scout hike. Standing (left to right): Herbie Frank, Bobby Gersh, Arnie Rosen, Monroe Korn, Donny Robins, and Bernie Kastenbaum. Kneeling: Harris Goldstein with Harold Rosen. Photo taken on Surf Avenue in Sea Gate, 1947.

Friendships: Cliques, Clusters and Hierarchies

Friendships evolved at every stage of growing up in Sea Gate. As young pre-nursery children, we were thrust together by the geographic boundaries of our block. Don Robins lived upstairs and was my closest friend then and today. Down the block were Bernie Frank, Phil and Len Friedman and on the first street inside the Gate were Bart Meissner and Harris Goldstein. As we grew older, relationships waned and new ones formed. Shep Finkelstein (now Forest), son of a lawyer, became the titular head of a new circle of kids on the next block, which included Bernie Kastenbaum (now Kasten), Morty Blum, Carl Levine, Robert Summer, Eddie Feinberg, Rich Oberfield, Harvey Weiss and Morty Gross.

Robert Summer (left) and Shep Finkelstein (right). Circa 1945.

(Bottom to top): Carl Levine, Shep Finkelstein, and Rich Oberfield. Circa 1945.

A bar mitzvah reception at the Ocean Breeze Hotel. First row, left to right: Unidentified girl, Carl Levine, Robert Summer (unidentified boy in front of Robert Summer), Eddie Feinberg, Morty Gross. Second row: Eli Flam, Harvey Weiss. Third row: Morty Blum, Bernie Kastenbaum (head bowed, picking a pocket), Donny Robins, Rich Oberfield, and Shep Finklestein, circa 1945

Within the group there were widely different personalities, attitudes, and loyalties. Typical of adolescent rite of passage, they indulged in teasing and trifling raillery directed at a "candidate for the day." For whatever reason, I seem to recall that I was the recipient of more than my fair share. Most went along with the mostly benign taunts and jeers. If anyone perceived that it might be hurtful, they kept silent, not wanting to disrupt their standing with the group. However, each one, when isolated from the group and not compelled to perform, could engage in a friendly and sincere conversation. There was never any parental intervention and we would hold no long-lasting grudges. I recall one incident of "divine intervention." It was a snowy afternoon and our group was walking home from school. Someone decided to anoint Carl

Levine as the "candidate of the day" for attack—not a verbal attack but a snowball barrage. He suddenly was inundated with snowballs. Carl survived the attack unscathed but nonetheless was devastated and humiliated. The next day, Carl's older brother, Murray, confronted the alleged "ring leaders" and warned them, "Never again do this to my little brother, Carl!"

As I grew older different friendships evolved based on athletics. Our love for sports, especially basketball, brought a close bond with Eli Flam, Buddy Rubel, Marty Tankowitz, Norm Schwartz, Saul Weiser, and a Brighton Beacher, Alan Stein. We played basketball at the Riviera and softball at the tennis courts. Saul Weiser was a phenom as a windmill pitcher. I was his catcher and at the end of seven innings my hand was aching after catching his blazing fastballs. Eli "Ish" Flam, at 6' 2", was tall by 1949 standards. He was a multi-talented, gifted shooter and ball handler on the basketball court. Marty "the Gobe" Tankowitz and Norm "the Storm" Schwartz were scrappy and tenacious defensive standouts. Bud "Uncle Bud" Rubel was laid back didn't work up much of a sweat, but had a deadly one hander. Big, burly Alan Stein played with an infectious, perpetual smile, just happy to be among friends. Alan loved to visit Sea Gate not only for basketball but because he was infatuated with a Sea Gate girl. We soon grew as interested in girls as in athletics. Eli, Buddy Rubel, Saul Weiser, Alan Stein and I would sometimes get together with Laurie Frankel, Rhoda Eisenberg and Anita Kaskel to celebrate a "sweet sixteen" party or a similar social event.

Still Friends After All These Years

After high school most of us went our separate ways. It was not until Don Robins' wife, Beverly, made Don a fortieth birthday party in 1972 that I reconnected with my original Surf Avenue gang. We continued to keep in touch with periodic mini-reunions for birthdays, our children's bar mitzvahs, and other special occasions. Anita Kaskel-Blum invited us all to a gala black-tie fiftieth birthday party for husband Morty, and this was followed by a bar mitzvah celebration for Harvey Weiss' son and Bernie Kastenbaum's fiftieth birthday, a black-tie celebration at a loft in Soho. We reassembled once again for my son Paul's bar mitzvah in 1984.

I was still longing to hear from my athlete group of friends. After retiring, I had the luxury of time to search and reconnect with some of them after fifty years through the Internet. I found Saul Weiser living in Las Vegas, Marty Tankowitz in New York City, Eli Flam in Southern Maryland and Buddy Rubel in Philadelphia. It was a joy to visit Eli at his home in Port Tobacco, Maryland and Buddy at his summer home in New Hope, Pennsylvania. Their wives, Lucy Flam and Sue Rubel, were gracious hosts to Marylyn and me. The girls were also good sports as the guys spent most of the time reminiscing about our Sea Gate days at Buddy's also with Ted Arenson (married to Cynthia). These renewed friendships have been very heartwarming and evoked so many fond memories of Sea Gate at a special time in a special place in our lives. Sadly, I've lost three good friends who died too young: Alan Stein, Saul Weiser, and Rhoda Eisenberg.

Still friends after all these years. Eli Flam (left), Arnold Rosen (right) with Rhoda Eisenberg (center) circa 1950

CHAPTER 4

I REMEMBER

A nostalgic collection of narratives of our youth in Sea Gate

Arenson, Ted: Ted lived at 3746 Maple Avenue from birth in 1933 to 1951, when he graduated from Lincoln. Ted pursued a career in teaching and running a hotel with his wife in upstate New York. Ted is retired and living in Park Slope, Brooklyn.

Ted Arenson Photo: Ted Arenson, looking at one of his bar mitzvah checks at Moscowitz's Hotel on Surf Avenue, June 23, 1946.

I now perceive, although maybe not then, that Sea Gate back in the '30s and '40s afforded children therein both safety and a kind of almost absolute freedom, not readily available to most kids today. We roamed the confines of the Gate without worry and engaged our games on readily available appropriate spaces that had not yet been transformed into parking lots or post-war housing (although my first solo sojourn to the Surf Theater was accompanied by a parental promise to duck into the nearest air-raid shelter if the Luftwaffe should appear on the horizon).

The next best part of growing up in the Gate was its proximity to Coney Island and all that entailed—from classroom contact with a new bunch of guys and gals, to outfielder for the Sixtieth Precinct's 1949 City Champions, Coney Island Crackers, to my first real summer jobs at Katz's Penny Arcade, Bat'em and the Fishing Game—my final stop on my Coney Bowery Hall of Fame. From there, it was but a step or two up, or maybe down, the boardwalk to the bright lights and the heady temptations awaiting in that den of iniquity: Brighton Beach.

Brenner, Donald: Don lived at 3729 Lyme Avenue. He graduated Lincoln in June 1949 and attended the University of Bridgeport. He served as a lieutenant in the U.S. Army in Korea and was awarded the Bronze Star, the Purple Heart, and the Combat Infantry Badge. Don is retired and lives in Big Bear City, California.

Don Brenner is a member of the Community Arts Theater Society (C.A.T.S) of Big Bear Lake, California. Photo shows Don in role of Ali Hakim in Oklahoma

I remember the Sea Gate Chapel on Friday nights where we attended Troop 256 Boy Scout meetings. I enjoyed softball at the tennis courts, basketball at the Riviera, walking with beautiful tanned girls from Beach One to Beach Four and back again. I remember dances at the chapel when the girls would dress up in crinoline or shirtwaist dresses, but I don't remember which organizations sponsored them. I remember sitting on the stoop at the Whittier Inn on summer nights eating ice cream cones—but mostly, I remember the beautiful girls.

Flam, Eli: Eli lived at 4022 Surf and 3727 Mermaid Avenue. He graduated from Lincoln in June 1950. After leaving Sea Gate and graduating from Brooklyn College, he worked as a reporter/editor in Manhattan, New England and Puerto Rico, and as a foreign service officer in the Caribbean, South America, the USSR, and Spain. Eli edited and published *Potomac Review*, a literary journal, for almost nine years. He lives in Port Tobacco, Maryland.

Eli Flam

In the introduction, I mentioned a canoe trip with Joe the lifeguard when I was a beachnik teenager. We set out on a hot, sunny summer's day without a specified destination, slipping past Beach Four and Norton's Point with nary a word from Joe in the stern. Then he pointed the bow toward the narrows; after a while we were making our way through that storied passage in the midst of all sorts of seagoing craft. Soon we slid by the dock for the Staten Island Ferry, to which I'd ridden on my bike, and past Owl's Head. Still no word from Joe, so I kept paddling without a break, staying on one side as long as possible before switching to the other. And then, *mirabile dictu*, we were in the Gowanus Canal, sharing the murky water with huge, docked freighters whose hulls loomed like waterbound skyscrapers. Finally we came about and headed back to Sea Gate, a stroke at a time. When we slid up on the beach at last, I knew my back and arms would be stiff the next day, but Joe's warm smile and a little nod gave me a lift. The next summer, when I became a waterfront counselor at a camp near Albany, I was ready to take campers on a weeklong canoe trip on Lake George. But as plastic surgeon Dr. Kay would tell you, I should have worn a good hat, and slathered on plenty of strong sun block, going to the Gowanus Canal, and many another day in the sun. What did we—or our parents—know in those days?

After fifty years a reunion of "old friends." (left to right): Martin "Buddy" Rubel, Eli Flam, Ted Arenson, and Arnold Rosen, New Hope, Pennsylvania, June 2, 2001.

Frankel-Feuerman, Laurie: Laurie lived at 36 Tudor Terrace and graduated from Lincoln in June 1952. She attended Brooklyn College and Adelphi University. Laurie is semi-retired and works as a speech pathologist and consultant. She lives in Hilton Head, South Carolina.

Laurie Frankel

Sea Gate, the name always calls back wonderful memories. It was a very special community—small, intimate, the beach and of course—the boys. I remember when I was young, I loved going to Beach One. We would plunge into the water and then roll around in the sand to warm up. Of course, there were always lunches sent along with just enough sand in-between the bread to remind you where you were. As I grew a little older and the beach was taken over by the army, we would go to the unoccupied areas looking for Nazi submarines. To our amazement, we did discover a huge crate of mayonnaise washed ashore! That was a real find in the days of rationing. We gave some of it away to all our friends and, of course, hoarded the remainder.

Probably the most significant memory is the evenings' biking to the Whittier Inn. We would hang out and just hope that one of the boys from "Sheppie's Gang" would notice us. *Gang* is kind of a funny term for a group of cute, well-scrubbed Jewish kids living in probably the most insulated environment. I think the only times we saw more Jews was when we left the gates of our protected enclave. In any event, the growing up and growing away were the sweetest moments of my life. If only one of those boys would have noticed the skinny, frizzy-headed girl with sand in her toes!

Freedman-Most, Irma: Irma lived at 3921 Lyme Avenue from 1940-1951. She graduated from Lincoln High School in January 1951 and Hunter College in 1955. Irma is a retired elementary school teacher who lives in New York City and Lords Valley, Pennsylvania.

Irma Friedman-Most

I lived in Sea Gate for eleven years (1940-1951) and the memories linger on. Despite my parents "depression mentality" and a world war, my childhood memories are filled with joy and my adolescent years exciting and adventuresome. My greatest legacy of having lived in Sea Gate is everlasting friendships and stories.

The war years were exceptionally memorable to me. We were encouraged to go to the Sea Gate Chapel and participate in various activities. I learned to crochet and knit Afghans, roll bandages and sew baby smocks and hats. I pulled my red wagon up and down Lyme Avenue collecting newspapers and tin cans for the war effort.

I remember romping on the beach, climbing on the rocks, fishing from the jetties and exploring the *Sylph* ferry. I recall watching Ethelind Altman turn cartwheels on the beach under the watchful eyes of the boys and the jealous gazes of the girls. We also "hung out" at the Sweet Shop and the Whittier Inn and enjoyed their ice cream treats with friends.

Goldberg, Eugene: Gene lived at 4208 Manhattan Avenue and at 3920 Cypress Avenue. He graduated from Lincoln in 1946 and attended the University of Illinois, playing varsity basketball for both schools. He served in the U.S. Army during the Korean War and worked as sales and marketing manager for Case Paper. Gene is retired and living in Manhasset, Long Island.

Gene Goldberg at Sea Gate Reunion, Boca Raton, Florida, 2002. He is seated with his sister, Barbara Goldberg-Furman (at left) and wife, Joanne,

I have such fond memories of the yacht club and the long pier where ferry boats would take Sea Gaters to Manhattan. After that service ended we would fish off the pier and catch plenty of fluke and flounder. I also recall the trolley cars that ran through the Gate and as we lived on Manhattan Avenue, the trolley went behind our house.

I vividly recall when it snowed and we attached ropes to the rear of the buses and glided through the snowy streets while the bus pulled our sleds. Sea Gate for me was an idyllic place. All the kids, on ball fields, summer at the beaches—Beach One was the favorite. Then there was the lighthouse— probably one of the oldest around. I remember all

the huge ocean liners sailing past us, especially in
the summer when we were on the beach and the
huge waves they created that swamped the beaches

Goldstein-Reinken, Martha: Martha lived at 3738 Maple Avenue.
She graduated Lincoln in January 1947 and attended the Parsons
School. Martha is a talented artist and has been the recipient of many
awards. She has shown extensively is solo shows in New York and
Connecticut. Martha lives in Greenwich, Connecticut.

**Martha Reinken-Goldstein. Martha at 16 on the
rocks at Beach One, circa 1946**

I remember going to the chapel on rainy days
in the summer and watching Charlie Chaplin's
silent movies there when we couldn't go to the
beach. We went to the beach everyday during the
summer. A lagoon formed on Beach Four near the
rocks and I loved just to sit in the calm water there

without any waves. One summer there was a tidal wave that swept over the beach and flooded the streets from Atlantic Avenue to Gravesend Bay. I remember the Riviera and how romantic it was. We youngsters would watch the older kids dancing to Cole Porter's music from the jukebox. The colored light bulbs were strung out overhead across the beams as couples danced on the deck with the Atlantic Ocean in the background.

As I rode the Norton's Point trolley, I would look into the windows of the apartments along the tracks. There were flower boxes on the windowsills. During the summer, their windows were open and I could hear the beautiful music and smell the aroma of olive oil, tomato sauce and garlic cooking on the stove. Inside the trolley, the seats were wooden slats. They gave us a transfer on the trolley to the subway so that we could ride to Manhattan for free.

Greenstein-Krown, Evalyn: Evalyn lived at 4409 Atlantic Avenue. She graduated from Lincoln in June 1950 and Hunter College in 1954. Evalyn was a teacher and lives in Westbury, New York.

Evalyn Greenstein-Krown

When I think of Sea Gate, I think of seasons.

Summer gives me my earliest memory, taking my towel and my red tube and walking across the street to the "lagoon" on Beach Forty-fourth Street, where I stayed until lunchtime. I remember Mello Rolls at the Whittier Inn, summer tenants, the iceman, and the produce truck of Johnny Judice and his father with a horse-pulled wagon and later on a truck. A pink Spaldeen ball made you the queen of the stoop. I would walk to the ferry with my mother to meet my father.

I recall the war years with the army encamped on the beach, waking up at 7 A.M. to the sounds of the troops marching down Atlantic Avenue to the mess hall with the German shepherds barking, the boom of the big guns going off during the afternoon practice, the canteen on Forty-fifth Street where my parents were volunteers, supplying sandwiches and pies from Messing, the lighthouse and its rotating beam of light that put me to sleep every night, the cargo ship that was beached on Forty-fifth Street, dances in the chapel, walking to school in the winter of 1947 after the blizzard and finding it closed. When I came home and told my mother, she told me that school is never closed. There was a ritual of Saturday matinees at the Surf Theater. Eleven cents admission, four cents to buy Indian nuts to last through two movies, Movietone News, two cartoons, and the serial— what more can anyone want?

Greenstein, Stanley: Stanley lived at 4409 Atlantic Avenue from 1937 to 1949. After graduating from Lincoln he entered CCNY in 1942, enlisted in the AAF as an air cadet in 1943, became a second lieutenant in 1945 and flew P-40s during the war. After the war, Stanley attended Harvard University. He is retired and living in Aventura, Florida.

Stanley Greenstein: Photo: Sea Gate Reunion, Boca Raton, Fl., February, 2001

While growing up in Sea Gate, I enjoyed school, playing football, and swimming at the Sea Gate Beach. I was a member of the Boy Scouts, and enjoyed attending services at Congregation Kneses Israel on Nautilus Avenue.

Harnett-Weil, Barbara: Barbara lived at 3907 Lyme Avenue. She graduated from Lincoln in June 1945 and received a Bachelor of Science degree from Cornell University in 1949. Barbara has three children and one grandchild and lives in Stamford, Connecticut.

Barbara Harnett-Weil: Barbara Harnett, a telephone operator at Gershonoff's Ocean Breeze Hotel

I remember Hazel and Adolph Weiss' home on Ocean View Avenue. The backyard faced the bay and was equipped with a davit (a device for raising and lowering a small boat). The house originally belonged to people who bootlegged during prohibition. Ships would come into the bay and row boats would be sent out to unload cases of liquor that were distributed to speakeasies. Lindy Park was next to the Weiss home. The guys played touch football during the day and at night they parked and necked with their dates. Other kids would then shine flashlights into the cars to startle the occupants.

My father took the *Sylph* to Manhattan instead of riding the subway. It was forty cents a ride and was convenient for him because he worked on Williams Street in lower Manhattan. I remember the Levine family on Atlantic Avenue. There were nine children, six girls and three boys—Murray, Carl, and Bobby. Everyone from Sea Gate was a friend with at least one of the Levine kids. Mrs. Levine always wore high-heeled shoes (the family owned a shoe store) and was always dressed up and looked as if she hadn't a care in the world. I had so many wonderful friends growing up in Sea Gate—Irma Goldman, Pearl Levine, Paul and Jack Berg, Bubbles Silverman (Beverly Sills), Bobby Horowitz, and Gloria Harnick. In 1976 we returned to Sea Gate to view the "Tall Ships" celebration. Our friends from Westchester were amazed that Sea Gate was so small and yet, so many people originated there. Wherever we traveled worldwide we always met people from Sea Gate

Author's note: This celebration took place on July 4, 1976. An international flotilla of warships sailed under the Verrazano Bridge into New York Harbor and more than two hundred high-masted sailing ships moved into temporary berths as Sandy Hook and Gravesend Bay in preparation for the city's sea and land bicentennial celebration. The coast guard reported that more than thirty thousand small boats were in the harbor area and around the tall ships off Sandy Hook. Most of these ships sailed by Sea Gate and Lenny Wachs erected a large "Welcome Sign" on the bulkhead near Beach Forty-sixth Street so that it was visible to the crews that sailed by.

Photo by Lenny Wachs for the "Tall Ship" celebration, July 4, 1976. Sign erected on the bulkhead near Beach 46th Street

Harnick-Blecker, Gloria: Gloria was born in Sea Gate in 1927 and lived at 3841 Maple Avenue until the mid-1940s. She graduated from Lincoln High School in 1945, attended Brooklyn College and then the University of Southern California where she got her degree. After USC she returned to New York where she worked in advertising for several years before marrying Herb Blecker in 1957. Gloria and Herb lived in Rye, New York, raised two children and have five grandchildren. From 1990-2002, she was on the staff of Congresswoman Nita Lowey, working in the White Plains District Office. Gloria died on March 19, 2003.

Gloria and Herb Blecker

My closest friends at Sea Gate were Barbara Harnett (now Weil), Bobby Horowitz (now Greenfield) and "Bubbles" Silverman (now Beverly Sills). My first boyfriend was Paul Berg. I remember growing up in Sea Gate and my wonderful days on the beach and my famous neighbors across the street—the actors Stella and Luther Adler. I loved eating clams at Lundy's on Emmons Avenue in Sheepshead Bay

Harnick, Robert: Bob lived at 3841 Maple Avenue, graduated from Lincoln High School in 1939 and attended the University of Alabama and Fordham University until 1942. He served in World War II in the signal corps of the U.S. Army. After the war he worked as a lithographer.

Robert and Sherry Harnick

Sea Gate was a wonderful place to spend a boyhood. It was like an "Everything Bagel" and Sea Gate can be called an "Everything Sea Gate" where growing up was like having it all. I remember so many favorite places and events: the Atlantic Yacht Club, the Mast of the Shamrock III, the *Sylph* that sailed to Battery Park from Sea Gate, Lindy Park and the glass battleship, the Norton's Point Lighthouse, hanging out at the Whittier Inn and the Riviera, crap shooting in the trolley car parked near the tennis courts, European liners causing massive waves on the beaches, cars towing sleds in the winter snow and the Sea Gate Gardens built by Donald Trump's father. I remember my friends: Jeep Rothman, Bernie Friedman, Beverly Sills, Augie Wolfe, Bob Rothstein, Issac "Iggy" Barkin, Al Goldstein, Gloria Finkelman, Ruby Raskin and Lenny Berkan.

"Behave, boys, or I'll take you down to the station." Sea Gate police officer Sid Zuckerman, warning (left to right) Jeep Rothman, Larry Kronenberg, and Bob Harnick, circa 1939.

When the war was over and I came home to my mother's house in Sea Gate, I knew that I finally arrived home because I could smell the sea air and hear the waves breaking.

Krown, Melvin "Sonny": Melvin lived at 4201 Sea Gate Avenue. He graduated from Lincoln in 1949 and Brooklyn Poly Tech in 1955. Mel worked as a professional civil engineer and is living in Westbury, New York.

Melvin Krown in Sea Gate, 1950

I remember a hurricane in 1938 when the trees in front of Benjamin Salzhauer's house and the rest of the trees along Laurel Avenue were uprooted.

On December 7, 1941, I was sitting on the steps of an old Victorian home across the street from where I lived on the northeast corner of Laurel and Sea Gate Avenue. I was with Alan Altman, Ronnie Berliner, Ronnie Teller, and Mel Cantor. The old house was vacant during the winter as it was strictly used for a summer rental. Someone discovered an open window and we decided to enter the house to explore. We made the rounds of the first floor, climbed back outside, decided to go to lunch and return later that afternoon to explore the basement. After lunch we returned with a flashlight and while in the basement, the cellar door opened and big Sgt.

Jim Maloney of the Sea Gate Police appeared. He herded us into his police car and threatened us about the penalties of breaking and entering. He mentioned taking us to the Sixtieth Precinct but decided to take us to my parents' home instead. He parked his car and told us (five crammed in the backseat) to wait. He never came out of the house. It seemed like forever. He finally came out with my mother and father, their faces were somber and I figured I would get "the beating of my life." It was December 7. The Japanese had attacked Pearl Harbor and our little incident was meaningless compared to the horrific event of that day.

Levine-Natter, Judith: Judy lived at 4304 Highland Avenue. She attended the Dalton School in New York and finished up at Lincoln. She lives in Houston, Texas.

Judith Levine-Natter when she was 15 years old.

I remember attending PS 188 from 1937 to 1942. My favorite teachers were Mrs. Wiesenthal (kindergarten) and Mrs. Marcou (third grade). My best friends then were Steve Sultan and Grace Ricken. I remember going to the Surf Theater to see one of my favorite movies, *Fantasia.* I remember my father taking me with him to check on a new baby he had delivered. The baby had been born prematurely and was the smallest thing I had ever seen. Alfreda Baker—she lived across the street from us on Lyme Avenue.

Lipson-Altman, Diane: Diane lived at 3829 Nautilus Avenue and graduated from Lincoln in 1946. She lives in Hallandale, Florida.

Diane Lipson-Altman Photo of Diane taken at Sea Gate Reunion, Boca Raton, Feb., 2002

I remember one winter when Lenny Wachs and some of his friends built a long wooden sled with fat wooden runners, and added a long rope they found on the Sea Gate beach near the Riviera. At the first snowfall they dragged the sled to the Surf Avenue Gate, waited for the bus, and looped the rope of the sled around the rear bumper of the bus. Then we all crowded on the sled. The bus took off and we went flying around Sea Gate on the sled in the snow, choking and laughing as we inhaled the noxious fumes from the bus exhaust. Boy, did we have fun!

Lipson-Hochman, Naomi: Naomi Lived at 3829 Nautilis Avenue (next door to the Sans Souci). She graduated from Lincoln in 1952, attended Brooklyn College and William Patterson University. For the past thirty-two years, Naomi has been as an educational consultant for children with learning disabilities. She lives in West Orange, New Jersey.

Naomi Lipson-Hochman

I remember the kids on the street played "Three Feet off to Germany," "Red Light," and "Kick the Can." We stayed out all day until parents started calling their children in for dinner. Tuesday night (in the summer) it was the boardwalk for fireworks with my dad. PS 188, Mark Twain, and Lincoln High! What great memories! My best friends, Rhoda (Eisenberg), Florence (Needle), Laurie (Frankel), and Anita (Kaskel) never seemed to have any fears in the Gate and always found something to do. We would meet at each other's homes, walk all over the Gate and talk for hours. We often sat on Beach Four in early spring and looked for submarines or went to the Surf Theater for Saturday matinee, which included two films and a *Superman* serial, cartoon, and *Pathé News*. I remember, on the weekends we sometimes went to Steeplechase in Coney Island or ice or roller-skating at the Prospect Park Rink. When we were older we ventured into Manhattan. Ice cream was always a favorite at the Whittier Inn or the Sea Gate Sweet Shop, where for an extra penny; I would get sprinkles on my ice cream cone. The bakery shop just outside the Gate on Mermaid Avenue was where Rhoda and I would go for a Charlotte Russe when I had the extra change, after picking up a rye bread for my mother. As teenagers we went to Beach One where the "older crowd" hung out and women played mah-jongg, and we could get a Coke and a snack at the Riviera. Looking back, I remember being a happy kid, and feel fortunate that I spent all my "growing up" years in Sea Gate.

Marcus, Hank: Hank lived at 3821 Nautilus Avenue and 3780 Surf Avenue. He attended Lincoln and graduated from Miami High School in 1938. He served in the U.S. Navy during World War II. Hank lives in Plantation, Florida. At eighty-three he still rides his motorcycle and flies planes.

Henry Marcus leaning on his Indian motorcycle in driveway of 3768 Surf Avenue, 1946.

I remember living in three Sea Gate homes—on Nautilus, Surf and Beach Forty-fifth Street. When I was at Beach Forty-fifth Street, I would go down to the beach and find that it was full of large rocks. When the tide would come in, it would fill up and form a lagoon. The lagoon was a safe and ideal place to go crabbing and rafting. I remember the Sea Gate trolley. As kids, we referred to it as the "Toonerville Trolley."

Meyerhoff, Lee: Lee lived at 3840 Laurel Avenue (Birdie Wolff's triplex), then moved to 3724 Laurel Avenue. His family then bought the house at 4222 Surf Avenue (one block west of the Floridian at Beach Four). Lee now lives in Woodland Hills, California.

Lee Meyerhoff (right) with son and wife

I remember Beach One handball courts with the smell of Coppertone; the Whittier Inn after the beach in the summer; the soft tarmac on the hot summer days; freezing winter winds coming up Mermaid Avenue past Izzie's Grocery and Fish Market; stealing candy bars from Stoller's Candy Store just outside the Neptune Avenue Gate; the freezing walk to PS 188 and the classroom of Mrs. Marcou, the art teacher who used to throw chalk or erasers at class disrupters; the *Sylph* and *Sylph II* anchored off

Gravesend Bay. I remember during WWII, and blackouts (my father was an air raid warden). I remember the hurricane of 1945 when all the trees along Laurel Avenue got blown down.

Needle-Halpern, Irene: Irene lived at 3716 Oceanic Avenue. She graduated from Lincoln in January 1947 and attended Parsons School of Design, and graduated in 1950. She is a painter and art instructor at the City College of San Francisco.

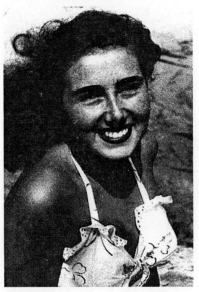

Irene Needle-Halpern

Sea Gate—one memory invokes another: redbrick sidewalks, maples, and sycamores; the Norton's Point trolley; the building of Tudor Terrace by Donald Trump's father, followed by the market, the Sweet Shop, and the barber shop facing Thirty-seventh Street. Memories of long summers, sunburns, and swimming, while watching out for Coney Island "whitefish"; watching ice skaters on the hosed-down and frozen tennis courts between Mermaid and Surf Avenues on cold winter evenings. There were playful seltzer wars among the teenaged boys—a prelude to the real war that would soon disperse them and thrust them brutally into adulthood.

Bess Lovinger's after-school art classes in her home at fifty cents a lesson included art supplies and were the high point of my week. We listened to Brahms, the A Train, and folk music; did homework; and jitterbugged; talked of our latest crushes on teachers, movie stars, and the boys at Lincoln. There was one Catholic family, the Contessas, in the Democratic Jewish stronghold of Sea Gate until Dr. Condello moved in. We were integrated!

Sea Gate was a nurturing place for kids. We all felt secure and protected venturing further as we grew older. How lucky we were!

Needle-Weingram, Florence: Florence lived at 3716 Oceanic Avenue with her older sister, Irene. She graduated from Lincoln in 1952 and attended Brooklyn College and Penn State. Florence was a speech and language pathologist. She is currently retired and lives in West Lafayette, Indiana.

I recall familiar houses and streets with nautical and tree names—Atlantic, Surf, Laurel, and Cypress. There are images of landmarks—the Sweet Shop, the Riviera, the Chapel, the Shul, the Ocean Breeze Hotel, and the lighthouse. I also remembered the old ferry boat at Gravesend Bay and deserted summer boarding houses that resembled haunted houses in the fall and winter. I can visualize the beach with its sand, ocean, rocks, and lagoon. We played in the snow and sledded down small hills on the empty lot between Oceanic and Nautilus Avenue before the "new houses" were built.

On walks or riding our bikes around the Gate we passed gardens with white, pink, and blue "snowballs" (hydrangea) and bushes of "bridal bouquets" (clustered little white spirea blossoms), hedges of privet and honeysuckle, peeling sycamore trees with "itching powder" balls below, maple trees with their sticky seed pods that we attached to our noses when we were younger, "weed trees" (ailanthus) with their mildly unpleasant aroma and sidewalks paved with red brick or repaved cement.

How privileged we were to live in Sea Gate. We grew up in a small community beside a phenomenon of nature and with easy access to the culture of a great city from which we were separated only by a protective gate.

Oberfield, Richard: Rich graduated from Lincoln in June 1949 and lived on Oceanic Avenue. He retired from his practice as a medical oncologist at the Lahey Clinic but continues to do research on cancer projects. Rich lives in Newton, Massachusetts.

Richard Oberfield

I recently was in New York for a short trip

and did visit Sea Gate. Quite a few changes! The area is really locked up and even pedestrians need to have a card to get in since now there are gates on the sidewalks with a slot for an ID card. The most shocking news was that my small house was converted into five apartments probably inhabited by five different families, all Hasidic Jews who now seem to predominate in Sea Gate. The large hotel across the street (Max Gershunoff's) is now a well-maintained senior citizens' home and the owner lives on my old street—Oceanic Avenue.

Powsner, Louis: Lou lived at 3807 Laurel Avenue and graduated Lincoln in January 1939. While at Lincoln he was the sports reporter for the *Lincoln Log* and school correspondent for Lincoln sports for *The Brooklyn Eagle*, *The New York Times*, the *Journal American*, the *World-Telegram* and *Sun*, and the *Herald Tribune*. Lou served in the U.S. Army Air Corps with the 494th Bomb Group during World War II. When he returned to Sea Gate after being discharged, he worked as a journalist and helped his family in the Powsner menswear store on Mermaid Avenue. Lou is retired and lives in Brooklyn.

Lou Powsner and bride, Irene on wedding day, April 14, 1946

We used to shoot craps in the trolley cars parked

alongside the tennis courts in Sea Gate. Some of the crapshooters were Murray and Freddie Kornfeld, Jerry Leibowitz, Howard Tapper and Murray Winter. One day the cops came into the trolley and broke up our game. They arrested us and brought us down to the Sixtieth Precinct on West Eighth Street. We were issued a summons and had to pay a $2 fine.

I enjoyed sitting on the beach and watching the big ships sail by—the Bremen, the Mauritania, and the Europa. I lived on Laurel Avenue and I used to walk to the beach barefoot—a macho, but foolish, thing to do. During the walk, the sidewalks were so hot we had to jump onto lawns to cool off our hot feet.

Rifkin, Gene: Gene lived at 4016 Surf Avenue, 3721 Nautilus Avenue and 3829 Oceanic Avenue. When he left Sea Gate he lived in Woodmere, Long Island. Gene now lives in Boca Raton, Florida.

Gene Rifkin

I remember and enjoyed playing softball on the yacht club grounds (after the fire); football on the tennis courts, swimming on the beaches and the lagoon; enjoying the company of good friends—Paul Berg (Noble Laureate), Beverly Sills, Sandy Levitt, and Sandy Levine.

Robins, Don: Don lived at 3780 Surf Avenue (seventeen years) and at 3800 Poplar Avenue (seven years). He graduated from Lincoln in June 1949. Don attended Syracuse University and its medical school. At Syracuse he earned an AB degree (magna cum laude) and an MD degree. Don served in the U.S. Air Force as an MD, with the rank of captain. When he returned to civilian life he set up a practice in pulmonary medicine in Westchester County, New York, later moving to Pittsburgh, Pennsylvania, and finally to Scottsdale, Arizona.

Don Robins

Appropriately named, Sea Gate was and is the gateway to New York Harbor. It is situated at the end of a peninsula, and had a prominent lighthouse at Norton's Point, which was a beacon for ships. I still can hear the sounds of the sea and remember dreaming of faraway places as the larger ships passed me as I played in the surf and sand. Now living in a gated community, which is quite common in the Phoenix area, I tell my friends that I grew up in one of the first gated communities in New York City. My love of gardening began in Sea Gate, where I experienced the sights and smells, in particular, of beautiful roses. The Ferbers, next door, had one of the nicest rose gardens.

The Sea Gate Chapel stands out as the headquarters of Boy Scout Troop 256. Here we met every Friday night and enjoyed the camaraderie of young boys and men working, learning, and playing together. In World War II, the troop did our job collecting newspapers, tin cans, and other objects used in the war effort. Finally, the various Sea Gaters continue to keep in touch at birthdays, and reunions, renewing our wonderful memories.

Rosen, Harold: Harold lived at 3780 and 3768 Surf Avenue and 4016 Atlantic Avenue. He graduated from Lincoln in June 1955 and attended Ohio State University. Harold lives in Tamarac, Florida.

Harold Rosen

From the fog of my early childhood, I remember the veterans coming home from WW II, playing softball in the tennis courts. I remember the trolleys parked across the street on Surf Avenue with their wooden slated seats that faced in either direction. We used to play in the abandoned cars before the watchman chased us away. I remember an old ship that was beached on the back bay of Sea Gate. I also remember, in the spring of 1948, a ship called *The Charles Tufts* ran aground not far from the lighthouse in a fog. It was a few months earlier, in December 1947, that Sea Gate (and the area) was pelted by one of the biggest snowstorms to ever hit New York. The older guys tied their sleds to the back of the bus and sleighed around the Gate. In November 1951 a fierce nor'easter storm hit the beach at Sea Gate with gale-force winds and record-breaking waves. This storm did a lot of damage to some of the beachfront homes along Atlantic Avenue. Our old home at 4016 Atlantic Avenue had a panoramic view of the beach and ocean. I remember watching the great ships and freighters sail by.

Schwartz, Noel: Noel lived at 4314 Sea Gate Avenue. He graduated from Lincoln in January 1945 and immediately enlisted in the U.S. Navy with his two friends, Anatole Shub and Elliot Usefuff. After the war he attended Columbia University and received a BS and MS degrees in science. Noel was president of U.S. Testing Company, an international firm. He is retired and living in Neponsit, New York.

Noel Schwartz: (Left to right) Elliot Usefuff, Noel Schwartz, and Anatole Shub in Sea Gate, 1946

I was not a jock and neither were my two close friends, Elliot Usefuff and Anatole Shub. Both their fathers were part of the Alexander Kerenski's cabinet when Kerenski served as president of Russia from July to October 1917. The families moved to Sea Gate in the 1930s and David Shub, Anatole's father, wrote extensively about the Russian revolution, an acclaimed biography of Lenin, and a 1930 article on Joseph Stalin in *The New York Times*. Anatole Shub, my best friend, wrote several books and later became Moscow correspondent for the *Washington Post*. The Shub family lived on Highland Avenue and his father raised and trained pigeons which he kept in a coop on his roof. I used to visit Anatole and remember seeing ten or more of his father's friends sitting around the kitchen table still plotting the overthrow of Stalin.

I served as best man at the wedding of my friend, Elliot Usefuff. Alexander Kerenski, the former president of Russia, attended the wedding.

Shapiro-Montella, Rhoda: Rhoda lived in Sea Gate from 1931 to 1953, at 3807 and 3740 Oceanic Avenue. She is retired and living in Delray Beach, Florida.

Rhoda Shapiro-Montella: At the beach: clockwise: Don Brenner, Joan Blum, Rhoda Shapiro, Morty Blum, and Herbie Frank, circa 1948.

As a child, I enjoyed the beach and playing squash on the handball courts at the Riviera. My parents would take me to evening dances at the Riviera and I enjoyed watching them dance under the stars. In the 1930s and '40s the 3700 blocks of Oceanic and Nautilus Avenues had many empty lots. These lots were not built up until the Waxman Homes were built after World War II, greatly increasing Sea Gate's population. My Sea Gate memories are a glimpse into a different world—a world where we never locked our doors; a world where I never carried a key; a world also where we knew Bill, the sergeant of the Sea Gate Police, would watch out for our house when we were away. Imagine that in today's world!

Shorofsky, Morris: Morris lived at 4408 and 4406 Beach Forty-fourth Street. He received a BA degree from Cornell in 1953 and an MD degree from the University of Basel in Switzerland in 1959. Morris served in the U.S. Army in Germany and is practicing medicine in New York City.

Morris Shorofsky

We lived on Beach Forty-fourth Street with a view of the Atlantic Ocean as it begins to narrow into New York Harbor. In the '30s our tenant in 4406 was the author, IJ Singer (*The Brothers Ashkenazy*), the older brother of Isaac Bashevis Singer. I have fond memories of viewing the ships entering and leaving the harbor and trying to identify them by their size, number of stacks and other distinguishing features. When the large passenger ships like the *Normandie* and the *Queens* would arrive during high tide the lifeguards did their best to get everyone out of the water before the huge waves flooded the beach.

Kite flying from the beach was a favorite pastime when the wind was right. Our next-door neighbor, Mr. Contessa of J. C. Yarn Company, kindly supplied us with spools of string. We would send messages up the string to the kite that was headed for China.

The beach also served the orthodox Jewish community faithfully. I fondly remember going with my father each Jewish New Year (*Rosh Hashanah*) to cast our sins in the ocean—the custom is called *Taschlich*. I doubt if it contributed to the eventual beach erosion. For years, Al was our favorite policeman who guarded our Beach Six entrance. When he was not checking passes he would teach us magic tricks. There was never any need to lock our front door. Sea Gate seemed to be the safest place to be.

Spodek, Sheldon: Sheldon lived at 3819 Neptune Avenue. Photo below was taken in the summer of 1943, on Beach One with girlfriend Rosalie Firester, longtime husband and wife and living in Delray Beach, Florida.

Sheldon Spodek

I recall when the heavy rains came and Sea Gate Avenue would flood, Lenny Wachs would take a small rowboat and help people cross the streets. I remember the name of the boat that took passengers to downtown Manhattan to work and returned home at night. What a wonderful cruise for only a half a dollar! The ship's name was the *Sylph*. I remember the snows of winter would remain until the April rains washed the streets clean once more. I remember Al Abraham (aka "The Prince of Peace") who sold the papers on Thirty-seventh Street where the trolley ended its run. I remember the wonderful Sweet Shop, on snowy days, where I would take my girlfriend for hot chocolate and an English muffin after a harrowing sled ride around Sea Gate, hitched to the back of the bus. I remember the horse that had a triangle box hooked up to him and he would walk on the sidewalks to level the snow on the streets

I remember the stores inside the Gate—the barber shop and Rand's Cleaning store. I remember bar mitzvahs at the shul where the women sitting in the balcony would throw down candy to the bar mitzvah boys. I remember Rabbi Ezra Gellman and Mr. Leibek who presided over my bar mitzvah and also at my wedding when I married my Sea Gate girlfriend and wife of fifty-five years, Rosalie Firester of Cypress Avenue.

Steinberg-Gerst, Gloria: Gloria lived at 3809 Maple Avenue from 1927 to 1947. Her mother grew up in Coney Island when it was farm country; her parents moved to Sea Gate soon after they were married. Gloria's father was president of the Sea Gate Association. Gloria is retired and living in Florida.

Gloria Steinberg-Gerst

Some of my wonderful memories of a Sea Gate childhood include riding my bike up and down Highland, Surf and Atlantic Avenues to visit my friends and always feeling very secure; going to the lot at the old yacht club near the pier and watching Sunday morning ball games; meeting my father at the pier in summer when he and many other residents came home from Manhattan on the *Sylph*, which commuted to and from Sea Gate to lower Manhattan; going to the beach to meet friends; spending time with friends on the Orioles and Sabers teams, and even helping my brother coach the Sabers; enjoying a walk to the Whittier Inn for ice cream in my younger years and then later to the Sweet Shop, where I took my husband on one of our first dates.

I had a wonderful childhood and I think living in Sea Gate contributed to it immensely. I had many friends and an extended family and I seemed to get good vibes everywhere in the Gate.

Stern, Jerry: Jerry lived at 3842 Neptune Avenue. He graduated Lincoln in 1953, Brooklyn College in 1958, and Syracuse Law School in 1963. In 1974, Jerry accepted the position as administrator and counsel of the State Commission on Judicial Conduct, which he has held for the past twenty-nine years. He lives in White Plains, New York.

Jerry Stern with grandson Jared, 2002

As a child growing up in Sea Gate, I could not imagine living anyplace else. In the 1940s, there was no greater thrill for me than to return from school, change into play clothes and get to the streets to play punchball—a loose version of baseball played with a small, pink soft ball, called a "Spauldeen," touch football, or games patterned after hide-and-seek called "Kick the Can" and "*Core Core Ringalevio.*"

During the war years, the Sea Gate beach was taken over by the U.S. Army. My friends and I plugged our ears, and watched the soldiers fire the big guns into the Atlantic Ocean, and when the firing was done, we scooped up spent shells. With all the soldiers stationed there, I was able to compile quite a collection of army insignias, which my mother sewed on my favorite jacket. She was a volunteer at the canteen on Atlantic Avenue, which served food to the soldiers at night.

After the war, Sea Gate's summer sport of prominence was softball because for some reason this small community could field a team of guys in their 20s and 30s who competed with the best amateur teams in New York City. Sundays at the tennis courts was a special spectators' sport for me as I watched the "older guys" play semi-pro teams. Among the most prominent was the Harlem Yankees, an all-Black team of great athletes, with the famed Tommy Long pitching windmill. Our guys, Ray Shore, Lenny Wachs, Jerry Liebowitz, Kenny Sommer, Irwin Plattman, Dave Glickman, and Monroe and Howie Adler were my heroes, ranking in hero worship with the Brooklyn Dodgers. Adult spectators would pool money to match the funds that the visiting team came with- winner take all.

In the early 1950s, my teen years, I would join friends on a football and softball field, known in Sea Gate as the *tennis courts* (there had been no tennis courts there since the 1920s or 1930s) or at the handball courts for handball, fast-pitch stickball and basketball.

In summer months, we had the beautiful Sea Gate beach, where we began the day playing "Triangle," a game patterned after baseball, but played on the hard sand. The "batter" would select a pitch bounced to home plate by the other team's pitcher and try to slap the Spaldeen between the opposing team's infielders. If the infielder fielded the ball, he had to get the ball to first base before the batter arrived; if the batter beat the throw, he was safe at first. If the batter hit a ground ball past the infielders, he had a double, triple or home run. We created the foul lines by drawing them in the hard sand, and the game could be played only in the mornings or other times before the tide came in and washed away the base paths. In the afternoons, we baked in the sun, swam, and "rode the waves."

I recall thinking how lucky I was to grow up in Sea Gate. Summer camps were for rich kids from other neighborhoods. We didn't need summer camp. In the evenings, we strolled the boardwalk in adjoining Coney Island, spent some money at the amusement parlors on the boardwalk, but if it was Tuesday night, it was time to eat French fries and watch the famed Coney Island fireworks. I'd never miss a Tuesday night on the boardwalk.

After spending two decades in Sea Gate, I left for about ten years, but returned in the late 1960s for nearly two years with my wife and two children.

My favorite home movies of my children are those of their playing on the Sea Gate beach, in the yard near our home, and on the Coney Island amusement park rides. I have been out of Sea Gate for more than thirty years, and I still miss it.

Tannen, Robert: Bob lived on Beach Forty-sixth Street across from the lighthouse.

This photo of Robert Tannen and two daughters were taken by his former (and deceased) wife, Barbara Orans at their home at 4715 Surf Avenue in 1959. Daughter Billie is on the right and Erica is on the left.

The recollections of my early life in Sea Gate include surfcasting and courting on the jetty at Norton's Point. The ensuing courtship resulted in the merging of the Tannen and Orans families through marriage to Barbara Rose Orans, daughter of Francis and David "Ury" Orans Jr. and granddaughter of Regina and David Orans Sr. The Orans family lived in stately homes along Surf Avenue, which were influenced by the prominent architect Stanford White.

Adrian Bouvier was my first friend in Sea Gate. His family was French-Canadian. He had one of the first TV sets in the neighborhood and attended Our Lady of Solace Catholic School in Coney Island. My friend Barry Yampol lived next door along with the Pincus and Rabb families. Other families in the neighborhood were the Rubinstein, Goldstein, Warshaur, Levine, Wise, Albert, Pollack, Kaskel, Saloff, Altman, Weinstein, Duberstein, Daar, Leibowitz, Ogler, Wortman, Schwartz, Costello, Zucker, and the Garmacy family.

Wachs, Leonard: Lenny graduated Lincoln in 1944 and still lives in Sea Gate.

Lenny Wachs at bat at the Sea Gate Tennis courts, circa 1943

I loved softball. It was my favorite sport. We played in the empty lot near Lindy Park and at the tennis courts on Surf Avenue. Our team was called the Royals and our uniforms were red and white. The team roster included Monnie and Howie Adler, Ray Shore, Dave Glickman, Kenny Sommer, and the Schechter brothers. My father and I built the stands and erected the scoreboard for the Surf Avenue field. The competitive spirit and thrill of playing top-notch teams was exciting for me and for the Sea Gate spectators that filled the stands every Sunday. We played teams from

Harlem, Queens, and the best from the neighborhoods of Brooklyn. Ray Shore and Kenny Sommer were outstanding players.

The Ship on the Beach: A Special Remembrance

When I was young, I lived near the beach. My beach was at the beginning of the harbor of New York City. My street ended at the water and right there at the end of the street was a tall, white lighthouse. All night the lighthouse would shine a red light to warn the ships,

"Stay away, stay away. The water is not deep here and there are rocks. If you come too close, you will get stuck in the sand of the beach and in the rocks. Stay away."

The light turned all night. First it was shining out to the ocean, then on the beach, and then on my street and its houses. Next it would shine on my house and my bedroom was filled with red light. It kept turning and the light went to the other side of the beach for a little while. Next the light was shining out to the ocean and the whole thing went on again and again. Every ten seconds the light made its turn. I liked it when the light came into my room because it meant that everything was safe and good.

If there was fog on the water, the lighthouse blew its foghorn every ten seconds, too. That way the sailors on the ships could hear the horn and knew that there was danger even when they could not see the light. I liked the sound of the foghorn, too.

One morning, I woke up early because my bed was shaking. The whole room was shaking. The house was shaking. My mother and father told me to get dressed quickly and we ran out of the house. All our neighbors were in the street. We were afraid that something terrible was going to happen. We thought our houses would fall down.

Someone came from the beach and said, "It's on the beach!"

We all ran down to the beach. On the beach we saw a big ship. It was stuck in the rocks and sand of the beach. It looked very funny and very big. The sailors were trying to back out of the rocks. The engine of the ship was making a lot of noise. The engine was making the beach shake. That was why my house was shaking. We told the sailors to turn off the engine. They said, "The powerful engines cannot get us out of here and we will turn them off."

It was nice and quiet and we talked to the sailors. They sang songs in another language. They had money and candy from other countries and they threw the coins and candy to us. It was fun.

The next morning my bed was shaking again. I got dressed quickly and ran to the beach. The engine of the ship was going again and it was trying to back the ship out of the rocks. This time, there were two tugboats helping. Big ropes from the tugboats were tied to the back of the ship. The tugboats pulled and the engine of the ship roared. The tugboats blew their whistles and the sailors on the ship rang a bell and blew the ship's horn. One of the kids on the beach said, "Look, it's moving!" Yes, it was starting to move. At first it went very slowly and then it started to move faster. It was getting free of the rocks. After a few minutes, the ship was in the deep water.

A loud blast from the ship's horn told the tugboats and us that the ship was able to sail by it. We all cheered and waved goodbye to the sailors. The tugboats blew their whistles a few times. We cheered for the tugboats. Then the tugboats and the ship turned to the city and sailed away.

We all wondered how the sailors made such a big
mistake. They steered the ship to the lighthouse instead
of away. Maybe they didn't know that our lighthouse
was warning the ships to stay away. It was lucky that
the rocks were there to stop the ship because it would
have hit the lighthouse.

We never saw the ship again but we always
remember it. We remember it because we see the place
in the rocks where it got stuck. And that place will
always be there.[9]

Richard Rubinstein

This narrative pertains to a ship that ran aground on April 26, 1948, on the rocks at Beach Forty-fifth Street. The *Charles Tufts*, a 7,176-ton freighter, was approaching New York Harbor when it apparently lost her bearings in a fog and grounded on the beach. Richard Rubinstein accurately describes the impact of the grounding as it shook houses in the neighborhood.

Anita Kaskel lived with her family at 4505 Beach Forty-fifth Street. She was fifteen years old at the time and was shocked to see the big ship outside her window. She shouted to her parents, "Look, look! A ship is in front of the house!" The family put on robes and slippers and went to the beach and joined hundreds of other spectators staring at the errant Liberty ship. The ship was even visible to motorists on the Belt Parkway, a mile and a half away, as it stood next to the stately Sea Gate Lighthouse. As strollers on the Coney Island boardwalk heard about the grounded ship, they headed for the West Thirty-seventh end and viewed the vessel from a half mile away.

The next day, with the help of five tug boats, the *Charles Tufts* was pulled free and sailed away from the Sea Gate promontory bound for the Todd Hoboken shipyard for repairs.

In Leonard Everett Fisher's *The Jetty Chronicles,* he juxtaposes reminiscence and imagination to weave a fascinating vignette about the actual ship grounding that took place in 1948. The date and the name of the ship are changed but he paints a fascinating word picture.

> One foggy wintry night in 1947, a year after I had left the army, we were all suddenly jarred loose from our beds. It happened to have been New Year's Day about an hour or two before dawn. The jolt was so explosive it sent shock waves through the house. Looking out the bedroom window I could see the massive bow of a twelve-thousand-ton "liberty ship," the *Charles E. Mason*, soaring out of the fog. I could almost touch it. House lights from all around—punctuated by the red beacon of the lighthouse as it rotated once every twenty or thirty seconds—threw an eerie halo around the ship's looming bow.

> The bow of the *Charles E. Mason* had practically gone through the bedroom window. The bridge and forward superstructure appeared to undulate in and out of the drifting mist. The rest of the ship lay hidden in the heavy fog and night. A lone figure holding the flashlight leaned over a railing to access the situation. A voice cried out from somewhere along the bridge. "Where are we, Mr. Swanson?" Back came the reply, "On the rocks, Captain."[10]

CHAPTER 5

A WALK UP MERMAID AVENUE

I remember, with affection, walking out of the protective confines of Sea Gate and strolling along Mermaid Avenue in the 1940s. In memory there were two or three luncheonettes on every block that sold everything from comic books to Charlotte Russes to frozen strawberry twist bars and Milky Ways. A thick malted with two large pretzel sticks became a favorite of kids in the neighborhood. The luncheonette (or candy store) was the true anchor of Mermaid Avenue.

The candy stores sold baseball cards with that awful slab of bubble gum, pistachio nuts in a glass bowl for one cent and a glass of seltzer for two cents. They had awnings with their name embroidered on the scalloped edges and signs provided by an ice cream (Borden's, Reid's, Breyer's) or a cigar company wholesaler, like Optimo. Outside the store was a wooden box that served as a newsstand. Stacks of *Daily News, Daily Mirror, The Times, Post, Journal-American, Brooklyn Eagle* and the *Forward* were held down by a steel rectangular weight to keep them from blowing away. Right outside the Gate, on West Thirty-seventh Street, was Sonny & Lou's Luncheonette. It was later sold and became Ann & Phil's.

Sonny & Lou's was the luncheonette my parents bought in 1951 and renamed it Ann & Phil's. I went overnight from a high school student, with outside interests in baseball, basketball, football, and music, to a student who worked in the luncheonette almost every hour I was not in school or sleeping.

I have never regretted and truly feel it was the right thing to do. The experience laid the groundwork for everything I have been able to accomplish in the years since the days of Ann & Phil's of Thirty-seventh Street and Mermaid Avenue. Arnie, I have not dwelled on this subject in many, many years, but thanks for giving me a chance to reminisce.

Steve Jackel

We used to sit in the back booth after our Friday night Boy Scout meetings in the Sea Gate chapel, looking forward to ordering their mouth-watering treats. Sonny and Lou worked behind the soda fountain. The fountain counter had a marble top and a row of revolving seats with a footrest attached to the base. There were three spigots with handles—one dispensed cold tap water and the other two dispensed seltzer. My friends would order ice cream sodas: all vanilla, all chocolate or black and white. Sonny also was a specialist in concocting sundaes or frappes mixing ice cream with syrup, whipped cream, and a variety of toppings. My favorite was their chocolate malted. After working up a thirst playing dodge ball (in the Sea Gate chapel), that filled-to-the-brim metal container of rich malted milk was pure heaven. Sokol's tailor shop was next door on West Thirty-seventh Street, and a pool hall upstairs where I would shoot pool with Eli Flam, Buddy Rubel, Norm Schwartz, Marty Tankowitz and Saul Weiser. It was operated by George (we never knew his last name), a part-time taxi driver, who enjoyed discussing politics, religion and the social issues of the day. Around the corner on Mermaid Avenue was Sally and Al's Delicatessen-Mer Restaurant with great hotdogs, sauerkraut and knishes. My friend Shep Finkelstein's aunt, Dr. Lena Finklestein, had an office on Mermaid near Thirty-seventh Street. She had a home in Sea Gate but spent most of her time in her combination office and apartment on Mermaid Avenue. Across the street was a beauty parlor, Bon Ton Cleaners, and Bucholtz, the butcher.

Bucholtz the butcher lived downstairs from my friend Irene Neal's house. My mother bought all her meats there. I remember the young Bucholtz used to sing: "Oy Oy, the butcher is Goy, Go get your money back, the butcher is a Goy."

I remember my mother bought schmaltz herring from Goldberg's appetizing store. When my parents had guests over the house, she would serve schmaltz herring and a glass of tea. The guests would place a sugar cube in their mouth as they drank the tea.

Martha Goldstein-Reinkin

I delivered orders for Bucholtz, the butcher. I remember the women customers would pick up a chicken, blow on it to make the feathers stand up in order to tell if the chicken was a plump or skinny bird. After they selected the chicken, the feathers were plucked by hand. When the customer got home the chicken would be singed to remove any remaining feathers. According to Kosher law, chickens could not be boiled to remove feathers or hairs.

Noel Schwartz.

My grandfather, Henry Lewis Schaffer, had a butcher store on Mermaid Avenue between Fifteenth and Sixteenth Street He made the hot dogs for Nathan's in 1916. The hot dogs cost Nathan 4½ cents and he sold them for a nickel. The drinks cost Nathan half a cent and he sold them for a nickel. The profit at that time was in the drinks.

Eddie Mann

Ironically, the only store that is still in business from the old days on Mermaid Avenue is a meat market—Major Markets. Jimmy Prince started working behind the counter back in 1949 and he is now the present owner.

Mermaid Avenue & W. 28th Street, circa 1953.
Photo courtesy of Andy Fuhrman

On the corner of Thirty-sixth Street was Backalenick's Drug Store. Drug stores also were ubiquitous along Mermaid Avenue. Magrill's Pharmacy was located at 3026 Mermaid and the Sea Gate Pharmacy at 3220. We would be able to buy aspirin, and over-the-counter medications from the stores without safety caps and hermetic seals then because no one had yet tried to poison a perfect stranger.

Near PS 188 was Backalenick's Drug Store. I recently met Mr. Backalenick's son at my gallery. We reminisced about his father's store. I reminded him that whenever I had something in my eye, I would go to him and he would skillfully remove it. I also

remember the long caramel lollypops we used to buy
on our lunch breaks from PS 188.
                    Martha Goldstein-Reinken

My dad died in 1929 and my mother kept the drug
store going. I'd sometimes work there after school for an
hour or two. One of my memories had to do with the
telephone. Very few Coney Islanders had their own phone,
so often a call would come in on the pay phone in the
store, asking if we could call Mrs. X or Mr. Y to the
phone. I would have to run across the street or a block or
two away and tell them they had a phone call. They
would put on their robes and slippers and come to the
phone. If I was lucky, I might get up to a nickel tip.
                    Bill Backalenick

Esther and Dick Stern's Luncheonette and Morris Ketchum's Grocery Store also shared the block on Thirty-sixth Street. The outside façade of the store featured Morris Ketchum's name on the awning and Salada tea, and Borden's milk signs on the windows. Ketchum's shelves were stocked with the usual cans and cereals and in the refrigerator case were blocks of fresh butter, carved to order from wooden tubs inside his glass-fronted icebox showcase. Cheese was sold in blocks or in cheese boxes of thin wood that were great to make toys or to store baseball cards. Transactions were simple for Morris. He would always have a short, stubby pencil held behind his ear. Morris would reach for the pencil, moisten the tip with his tongue and tally the prices on the side of a brown paper bag plucked from the stack under the counter.

When I relate this story to my friends from other neighborhoods, they say their grocer went through the same routine. It didn't matter whether the grocer was on Kings Highway, Avenue U, or Brighton Beach Avenue. Was there a school for grocers that instructed them to (*a*) keep a short-stubbed pencil behind your ear, and (*b*) tally the items purchased on a brown paper bag?

Walking up Mermaid Avenue, I remember Goldberg's appetizing store (at 3513 Mermaid Avenue) with the barrels of pickles outside and Mr. and Mrs. Goldberg behind the counter, wearing their white aprons and slicing Nova lox with the precision of surgeons. Further up on Mermaid Avenue was Rosenberg's Deli on Twenty-ninth and Greenwald's Kosher Deli on the corner of Thirty-second Street. They sold corned beef, Romanian pastrami and salami, which hung from the ceiling on a string. When we ordered take out, the mustard came in a wax paper cone, which was filled at the deli.

The Mermaid Theater was near Twenty-ninth Street. It was sometimes referred to as the "Itch."

> *The Mermaid Theater was located on Mermaid Avenue between twenty-eighth and twenty-ninth Streets, It was small compared to the other theaters and played movies after they had played in the local theaters. The air conditioning was a fan on the roof.*
>
> *On Saturdays, for ten cents, we saw a double feature, a chapter, cartoons, the news and a travelogue. In addition to the movies they gave you some cheap candy and sometimes ice cream. We went into the movies at twelve pm and did not come out until after five pm.*
>
> **Donald Picker**

The Surf Theatre, circa 1953. courtesy of Bob Greenwald

The Surf Theater was located on Surf Avenue and West Twenty-ninth Street. Both theaters charged ten cents for children and twenty-five cents for adults. We usually went on Saturday afternoon and saw a main feature, a Western, a newsreel, cartoons, and coming attractions. Candy was bought before we went in because it was five cents in the candy store and seven cents in the theater.

> *When the Surf Theater opened in the early '30s I handed out flyers that announced the upcoming movies. The owners would give me a free pass for the week. I remember I was watching a movie in the theater the night Bruno Hauptmann was executed for the kidnapping of Charles Lindbergh's baby. They blinked the lights off and on in the theater to signify that the execution was complete.* (Author's note: At 8:44 on the evening of April 3, 1936, in North Jersey State prison, two thousand volts of electricity were sent through Bruno Hauptmann's body.)
>
> **Lou Powsner**

Morris Weiner lived in Sea Gate. He owned a camera store on Mermaid Avenue. Nearby, Al Sinrod had a men's wear store on Mermaid and Twenty-seventh Street and the family also owned a tuxedo store on West Twenty-eighth Street.

Dr. Abe Levine, our family doctor, occupied a large white frame house on the corner of Twenty-fifth Street. Most of the doctors on Mermaid Avenue practiced general medicine and made house calls. Dr. Jacob Kravitz, another family practice doctor, lived with his mother in a private house on the corner of West Twenty-ninth Street. He drove a shiny black car appropriate for a doctor at that time.

> *I remember my Dr. Kravitz. He used to park his car on the street. There were few cars then and we played punchball and stickball on the street, deliberately avoiding touching or hitting his car. He*

was a man respected and we were in awe of him whenever he visited a patient. The neighborhood people knew his car and who was sick. He charged $3.00 for house calls and $2.00 for office visits in the 1940s. He treated me a few times for influenza and for second-degree burns from exposure to the bright sun when I played (unprotected) on the beach. When he walked into our apartment, he was always dressed with a dark suit and a starched white shirt, carrying a black bag. His very presence made me feel better. I had confidence in him. He had tongue depressors and instruments in his black bag. He looked in my ears, nose, throat, eyes, and listened to my heart and breathing. He integrated the information, made a diagnosis and usually wrote a prescription. My mother paid him in cash. He engaged in no small talk but when he left, I definitely felt better.

Sidney Krimsky

My aunt lived on West Twenty-third Street adjacent to Railroad Avenue, the right of way where the trolley would run. We would take a walk on spring and summer evenings on Mermaid Avenue to visit. Stores on Mermaid Avenue would stay open late. There was an A & P on Mermaid Avenue near West Twenty-ninth Street. My mother would buy the A & P coffee and have it ground it in the store. I remember the robust smell of the fresh ground coffee beans.

Mort Weiner

Dr. Hertzenberg, the optometrist, had a huge pair of eyeglasses mounted on the front of his store and visible for a few blocks. He was a big man with a smile to match his belly.

When we were seniors at Mark Twain and were allowed to go out for lunch, we would walk from Neptune Avenue to Mermaid Avenue to the Chinese restaurant and have their lunch special for fifty-five cents.

The Sea Gate Sisterhood and Talmud Torah and Yeshiva Shaarai Zedek (Gates of Righteousness) buildings were on the corner of Mermaid Avenue and West Twenty-third Street. The building entrance faced Mermaid and the top had an onion-shaped dome reminiscent of the design features used in Eastern Europe synagogues before World War II.

> *I attended daily classes at the Talmud Torah on Twenty-third Street, after dismissal from PS 188. When WWII ended, the Hebrew school students were asked to collect canned food for distribution overseas to help displaced persons. A classmate and I would pull a red wagon down Mermaid Avenue, walk down the side streets, knock on doors, and ask the residents for canned food. We trundled our wagon filled with canned goods up and down the elevator in the large apartment buildings, onto the street, and onto Mermaid Avenue, delivering the goods to the synagogue building.*
>
> **Sidney Krimsky**

I remember Kalistenik's Shoe Store on Twenty-second Street. They had a modernistic X-ray fitting devise that shoe stores used during the '40s. After we tried on our shoes, the salesman helped us onto a wooden box, which displayed our feet in the machine's viewfinder. The salesman would summon our parents to take a look into the viewfinder to see the distance between our toes and the front of the shoe to assure that there was plenty of room for growth.

> *My parents were friends with Aliza Greenblatt who lived in Sea Gate. She had a beautiful daughter, Marjorie, who was married, and was a talented Martha Graham dancer. At about the same time, Woody Guthrie, the folk singer, would often visit friends in their Mermaid Avenue apartments. Marjorie knew*

*about Woody's music and compassion for the
downtrodden. Both were cultural and political activists
and shared similar views. Her friend, Sophie Maslow,
who also was a Martha Graham dancer arranged to
meet Woody in New York City. When Marjorie first
saw Woody she was a bit shocked. She'd been expecting
a tall distinguished figure but found, instead a weird-
looking, disheveled man with unkempt hair and baggy
clothes. In spite of that a courtship ensued and Marjorie
and Woody were finally married. They rented an
apartment on Mermaid Avenue.*

Martha Goldstein-Reinken

**Woody Guthrie and Marjorie-Mazia Guthrie in
their apartment on Mermaid Avenue. Photo
Courtesy of the Woody Guthrie Foundation and
Archives.**

Together, Woody and Marjorie had four children: Cathy,
who died at age four in a tragic home accident; Arlo, Joady, and
Nora. In 1946, Woody Guthrie returned to settle in Coney Island,
New York, with his wife and children. Woody's behavior and
health became increasingly erratic and created tensions in his

personal and professional life. He left his family once again; this time for California and remarried a third time to a young woman named Anneke Van Kirk and had a daughter, Lorina Lynn. Woody suffered from Huntington's chorea, a degenerative disease and was in and out of hospitals for the next thirteen years. He finally succumbed on October 3, 1967.

> *I remember my sister, Rachel, was Cathy's age and they went to nursery school together. I also remember the fire in Woody's apartment. Marjorie grabbed Cathy, who was badly burnt and brought her to a local doctor on Mermaid Avenue. Tragically the doctor was not equipped to treat her severe burns and she died in the hospital. Before the fire, Woody would carry Cathy to the Casa D'Mor Nursery School. He would carry her on his shoulders and sing to her walking down Mermaid Avenue while my sister Rachel, and other kids would tag along listening to his songs. He would sing about the underprivileged and other social causes of the day. My family was involved in similar causes and we became close friends of Woody.*
>
> **Carol Weinshanker**

Joe Klein describes the trauma of that horrific day in his book *Woody Guthrie: A Life*:

> *When she returned, smoke was pouring from 3520 Mermaid Avenue. Arthur Young, the boy from upstairs, was there and he had a blanket. Then she saw that it was Cathy in the blanket and Cathy was gone. She was still alive, but she was just gone. The dress was gone.*
> *A doctor was summoned, the ambulance was there, and she was inside it with Cathy, who was semiconscious and whimpering, still in the blanket—and*

Marjorie did not have any idea what had caused the fire, or how it could have happened so quickly and do what it had done. She looked down at Cathy, whose face was the only part of her body that hadn't been utterly seared and even her face was beginning to blister, and she thought: Please, God, let her die. Don't make her suffer. Don't let her live like this.[11]

It was a treat to visit Woolworth's on Mermaid near Twenty-fourth Street. They sold everything from school supplies to cosmetics, clothing, and small hardware—all displayed on tables. They had little pads and crayons, notebooks, construction paper, and fountain pens. Ballpoint pens were introduced around 1946 and we still used liquid ink and fountain pens until ballpoint pens were available to everyone. More stores on the avenue included the Hubba Hubba Luncheonette on Twenty-ninth; Rand's Bar, where in 1946 we used to peek into the door when walking home from Mark Twain and look at the TV above the bar; Meyerson's Bakery on Thirty-third (for some reason there was no Thirty-fourth Street); Ann's Shirt and Zipper Hospital, and the Julliette Shoppe—all are gone and a distant memory.[12]

Day or night, during pre-adolescence or adolescence, I never feared for my safety walking along Mermaid Avenue. I used to window-shop especially in front of hardware stores. I was fascinated by the variety and ingenuity of all the tools and hardware I saw in the window.

Sidney Krimsky

In the 1940s almost all the food and clothing stores in Coney Island were on Mermaid Avenue. Surf Avenue had unheated bungalows for the summer people who came in June and remained until September. They would join the hundreds of thousands of people that streamed out of the subways on summer weekends filling the beaches and boardwalk.

Bathers crossing the tracks from the Coney Island beach between Mermaid and Surf Avenues. Photo courtesy of Robert Presbrey

In addition to customers from Sea Gate, the shop owners did most of their business from the nearby Coney Island residents. Families rented apartments above the stores and the entire cross streets from the Boardwalk to Neptune Avenue had apartment houses. Some were small, attached, yellow brick structures with porches up a stoop of stairs and basements below street level. The large apartment buildings were of brick and stood three or four stories tall.

> *I remember our first apartment when we were newlyweds in 1954. It was on the top floor of 3609 Mermaid Avenue. Most of the buildings on our street were similar. Our apartment consisted of three rooms and our rent in 1954 was $40.00 a month. Apartments were scarce at that time and we were glad to live there even though our landlord never provided enough heat in the winter.*
>
> **Carol Weiss-Weinshanker**

Joe Klein contrasts the two worlds of Coney Island—the

gaudy neon entanglement of roller coasters, fun houses, and merry-go-rounds with the residential part.

> But beyond the clangor, and largely unnoticed, there was a modest Jewish neighborhood—mostly garment workers, waiters, mom and pop storekeepers, poor people, drained and ravaged after fifteen years of war and economic crisis, living in shabby row houses on an earlobe-shaped peninsula jutting out into a filthy sea. New York's garbage washed ashore at Coney Island beach; the water was thick with condoms, bobbing along like so many jellyfish.[13]

The Prince of Peace

The shopkeepers and proprietors along Mermaid Avenue were a divergent group. Personalities and character traits ran the spectrum from highly animated to sedate businesslike demeanor. None of them was as eccentric as Al Abraham, the owner of a newsstand at the West Thirty-seventh Street terminus of the Norton's Point trolley. He sold newspapers and candy and dispensed his pseudo-religious rallyings to anyone that would listen. He was a character and would-be messiah and anointed himself, "The Prince of Peace." That's what the huge sign above the newsstand read. His signs were hand painted and included religious icons and timely phrases that he periodically changed. Hurried commuters who boarded the trolley did not have time to stop and listen to his preaching. They plunked their coins down for the *News* or *Mirror* and scurried off. His audience would have to be the non-rush-hour patrons that waited by his stand for the next trolley. Most listened, nodded and exchanged pleasantries.

Leonard Everett Fisher describes this colorful character in his book, *The Jetty Chronicles*. He calls him Jake Plaut.

Al Abraham's (The Prince of Peace) newsstand at the 37ᵗʰ Street trolley station. Courtesy of Robert Presbrey

Jake was the image of all those things he proclaimed to be. He wore his hair long—well below his shoulder blades. Deep black and well combed, it was held in place by a snow-white headband. Jake was bearded, too, beaded, colorfully robed, and sandaled. He was richly tanned, "from my many years on the desert," his description of the Coney Island Beach. No one could buy a newspaper from him without getting a softly spoken comment on love, brotherhood, sisterhood, peace, sinning, and doomsday.[14]

Leonard Everett Fisher

My father bought a building on Mermaid Avenue and Seventeenth Street across the street from the Catholic church. The ground floor was our family store, Powsner's Men Shop, and we lived in the apartment above the store. The Norton's Point trolley ran below my bedroom window. I remember Al Abraham, the "Prince of Peace," and his newsstand

*on West Thirty-seventh Street and around the corner
on West Thirty-seventh Street, was a junkyard owned
by the Michaelson family. They became very wealthy
buying and selling scrap metal during the war.*

Lou Powsner

Vendors in the Gate

There were a few stores inside the gate during the 1930s,
'40s and '50s. The Sweet Shop and grocery store were located on
Mermaid Avenue (inside the gate). Rose and Max Singer and
their sons (Jerry and Murray) owned and operated the grocery
store. It was called Met Food, Jet Food and other names from
1940 through the late '70s.

*Around the corner of the Sweet Shop there was
a beauty salon called Tiny's. Tiny was an Italian
woman, very petite and pretty with bleached-blonde
hair. She walked with a slight limp because of
chronic sciatica. My mother would always take me
to her shop for her standing appointment on
Saturdays. That place was a "torture chamber" for
me. I was five or six at the time and I dreaded
going there. My mother was obsessed with Shirley
Temple and she decided I should look like her. I
had straight hair and was pale and skinny. One
Saturday she took me into the shop for a makeover
with Tiny. I was put under a monster dryer with
heating attachments hanging down. I imagined it
was like sitting in the electric chair in Sing Sing.
To reach it they propped me up with telephone
books. After sitting under the dryer for hours my
wonderful hair emerged into Shirley Temple curls.
I thought I looked idiotic but my mother was thrilled.*

Teri Seidman

Danny Ginsburg and Barney Grabbler owned the Sweet Shop. It was a teen hangout and did a brisk lunch business during its hey days in the forties and early fifties. Home-cooked lunches were served to the Sea Gate locals as well as PS 188 students and teachers. Customers sat on stools along the counter and tables and booths were available at the rear of the store. During the evening, Sea Gaters would gather for late night snacks and ice cream treats.

Mickey Weinshanker worked as a counterman in the Sweet Shop in the early 'fifties. Eventually he purchased the store from Danny and Barney. He recalls his joys and frustrations as a business owner:

> *I remember working for Bill and Barney and Barney's family (his mother and father—Mom and Pop). They employed a full-time waitress, Catherine Alexander, (or "Kitty") a few part-time waitresses and countermen, but it was Willie, the cook, who was the "key man" in the business. Willie, an African-American, was the most loyal and reliable employee. He did the cooking and the customers loved the meals. Actually nobody knew that Willie did the cooking. They thought that Barney's mom did the cooking and the owners wanted to perpetuate that notion. Mom walked around the store wearing a "Schmutadikha" apron and she would greet the customers coming out of the kitchen. They all thought that Mom did the cooking. The customers would compliment Mom: "The mushroom and barley soup is delicious," "The brisket is out of this world today," "Mom, you have to give me your recipe for your chicken fricassee."*

Mickey recalls some of the local customers and their personality quirks. He relied on the regulars from Sea Gate as steady customers. Most were friendly and courteous. They enjoyed their meals and would often engage in conversation with

Mickey and his wife Carol. On the other hand he recalls the frustrations of dealing with others that were difficult, arrogant and demanding.

> *An old man would come in for a cup of coffee and read the newspaper that he retrieved from the stack. If he found something he liked, he would rip it out and stuff it in his pocket and then fold the paper up and return it to the pile. "Why do you let him do that?" Carol asked as she observed him from her cashier's perch. Mickey responded, "You know his sister-in-law, brother, his wife, they all come in here. If I confronted him about it he would get insulted, tell his family and I would lose the business. So I overlook it."*

> *Even worse, a judge who lived in Sea Gate would come in almost everyday. He would finish his coffee or lunch and walk over to the magazine rack and begin reading some of the pocket books that we have on display. He would stealthily pick up a book, place his overcoat over the book, pay for his meal, and walk out the store. He would do this on a regular basis. I asked him why he did tolerate this. "It's the price of doing business. Besides he helps me with my landlord tenant disputes and parking tickets."*

Mickey recalls the Sweet Shop's steady decline in the early 'sixties that finally shuttered the landmark store. Willie the cook retired, there was an excessive turnover of help and a rash of thefts—and the final "nail in the coffin" occurred when PS 188 went on split shifts and the lunch crowd was no more.

> *The lunchtime crowd from PS 188 gave us a big boost in business. We used to prepare dozens of hamburger specials—hamburger patties, French fries, and Coke. On Wednesdays we featured "Chin Lee"*

*chow mein and other Chinese specialties. Suddenly
PS 188 went on split sessions. Students attended from
8 A.M. to noon and another group came in from noon
to 4 P.M. There were no lunch periods. The kids ate at
home. We sold the business several months later.*

The Iceman Cometh and So Do the Chimney Sweepers

During the 1930s and 1940s many of the homes in Sea Gate
used iceboxes to refrigerate their food. Blocks of ice would be
delivered by horse-drawn wagons to residents. Vendors sold fruit,
vegetables, milk and dairy, products from their wagons and trucks.
Service-related vendors, such as dry cleaners, chimneysweeps, coal
delivery, and knife sharpeners, made periodic rounds servicing
the needs of the people inside the Gate. Hilly Multer was a
freelance glazier, carpenter, and handyman. He had a mild speech
impediment and always had a cigar in his mouth. "Buck, the
electrician" was also a Sea Gate freelancer who made the rounds
to service the needs of Sea Gate residents.

> *I remember Judice the fruit man and the Dugan's
> Cake and the Brighton Laundry trucks. Frank
> Matouri was the knife sharpener. He came around
> on a truck and sharpened the knives on a grindstone
> wheel, which he pedaled with his feet. He would finish
> his rounds in Sea Gate and ride up Mermaid Avenue
> sharpening the butcher's knives.*
>
> **Lenny Wachs**

> *I remember before the war years, many homes in
> Sea Gate used coal furnaces to heat their homes. The Sea
> Gate Association allowed selected men to collect the coal
> residue ash from furnaces. Horse-drawn wagons made
> the rounds to collect the ash and dump the residue into
> containers stored near Lindy Park. The biggest nuisance
> for the homeowners was to collect the ash, drag it up the*

cellar steps and place it out on the curb. Some ash collectors charged an extra fee to load the ash from the basement and carry it to the trucks.

Mel Krown

I remember the Judice family sold fruit and vegetables in a horse-drawn wagon inside the Gate. Judice was the first fruit-and-vegetable man in Sea Gate. He displayed his wares along the side of the truck and when he approached a street he would yell, "Fruit and vegetable man."

Evalyn Greenstein-Krown

I remember when the commuters came off the ferry from downtown Manhattan; an enterprising fruit-and-vegetable man parked his wagon outside the gate where the ferry docked. He cut a hole in the fence and the people coming off the Sylph ferry would buy fruit and vegetables from him on their way home.

Mel Krown

I remember when I was a teenager in the summers of 1947 and '48; I worked for Park Dairies delivering milk to Sea Gate residents. I arose at 1 A.M. in the morning and worked as a driver's helper from 2 A.M. to 8 A.M. Since the weather was very warm, the residents in Sea Gate did not want me to leave their milk outside on the porch. Instead they wanted me to bring their milk inside the house and place it directly into their iceboxes or refrigerators. They left their doors unlocked. Today it would be unthinkable to leave doors unlocked.

Stanley Davis

In the late '30s and '40 during my teen years, I lived in Borough Park, Brooklyn. My father, Louis

Blecker, was a "seltzer man" who had a truck with a route that brought him to Sea Gate every Tuesday to sell Good Health seltzer, Kirsh's soda and Fox's U-Bet chocolate syrup to the residents. During the summer, I was pressed into the service of helping my father and so I would enter Sea Gate every Tuesday. Sea Gate was surrounded by a fence and my father had to pay an annual license fee to pass through the "gate." It seemed to be an exclusive privileged community, where I thought then, only rich people lived. As we drove through many of the streets of Sea Gate—Lyme, Surf, Maple, Laurel, and Atlantic Avenues, we stopped every few minutes to make deliveries. I envied the kids who were running around, going to the beach and enjoying themselves while the sweat was running down my back carrying the heavy boxes of seltzer through the side entrances and up the narrow staircases to the second floor where we would drop off the filled seltzer bottles and take back the empties.

Although I longed to go on to the beach for a quick, cooling dip, we never had the time. Lunch was always at the Sweet Shop. I finally made it to the beach in July 1957 when my then girlfriend, Gloria Harnick, who grew up in Sea Gate and whose first boyfriend was Paul Berg, and was also a very close friend of Barbara Harnett (now Barbara Weil), took me there and to her home on Maple Avenue. We were married two months later and have had over forty-five wonderful years together, with two children and five grandchildren. Unfortunately, Gloria died on March 19, 2003, at the age of seventy-five after a bout with cancer.

Herb Blecker

My father used the Brighton Laundry for dry cleaning. I remember the big red truck and the driver, Mr. Goldstein, would make pick-ups and delivery every Thursday. He wore gray pants, matching Eisenhower-type jacket with "Brighton Laundry" stitched in script along the breast pocket, a cap and a black leather bow tie.

CHAPTER 6

THE WAR YEARS

Life on the Home Front

The Day of Infamy: December 7, 1941

> *Where were you on the afternoon of December 7, 1941? If your name was Michelle Piasco, you were at Carnegie Hall tightening the strings on your violin for the Sunday afternoon performance. If you were Gerald Nye, you were addressing 2,200 "America Firsters" in Pittsburgh. If your name is Suporo Kiroshi, you were waiting in the outer office of Cordell Hull in Washington, D.C. If you are a sailor named Tomash, you were at a place called Pearl Harbor where you and 2,116 of your buddies would be dead when the day is done.[14a]*

Like any American old enough to remember, most Sea Gaters can recall precisely where they were and what they were doing when the news came in that Japanese planes had bombed Pearl Harbor.

It was Sunday afternoon and I was sitting in the balcony, watching a movie at Loews Theater on Surf and Stillwell. Suddenly, the film was interrupted by an announcement over the loudspeaker and broadcast throughout the theater: "All servicemen report to their bases immediately." At that time, I was in the peacetime navy stationed at Floyd Bennett Field, so I left and reported immediately without delay. It was chaos! Navy personnel were running around in all directions trying to find out where to report and what to do. I was ordered to climb on the roof of Hanger 1, and with three other sailors assemble a 30-caliber machine gun on a tripod mount and stand lookout for possible enemy aircraft. None of us had machine gun weapon training, but we finally got it assembled after two hours.

Hank Marcus

On that day, I was on a weekend hike with Morty Sussman, Stanley Ferber and Jerry and Mel Silverman.

Sheldon Spodek

On December 7, a group of friends had been ice-skating at the Brooklyn Ice Palace. I returned to Sea Gate that afternoon to attend the first birthday party of Melvin Freedman, Irma's brother. All the people at the party were gathered around the radio in Irma's home on Lyme Avenue. They were saddened and very concerned about the loss of lives and what would happen to our loved ones who might have to go to war.

Don Robins

As I remember it, this 8-year-old was dozing in the backseat of our family car, a 1938 Plymouth. We were on the way home from an outing at my Uncle

Nathan's chicken farm in New Jersey, when word of Pearl Harbor came over the radio. I daydreamed about Japanese invading New York, with me and my pals riding our sleds downhill into bayonet-armed, charging soldiers and knocking them over.

Eli Flam

Sunday, December 7, 1941, dawned in Sea Gate—crisp, cloudy, and wintry. It was to be a day of joyous celebration, my brother Melvin's first birthday. My father drove to Mermaid Avenue collecting platters of food and at home, the doorbell kept ringing ushering in friends and neighbors laden with their homemade specialties—stuffed cabbage, noodle pudding, and gefilte fish. As the afternoon passed, the aura of frivolity changed. The men in the crowd turned on the radio hoping to hear the latest football scores. Instead, everyone heard the news that would change his or her lives forever— the Japanese had bombed Pearl Harbor. Mel's first birthday will always be remembered.

Irma Freedman-Most

On December 7, 1941 we lived on Beach Fiftieth Street near Lindbergh Park (later known as Kelly Park). My grandmother and I were the only ones home when the announcement came over our big Zenith radio about Pearl Harbor. My grandmother took my hand and told me to stand with her next to the radio as they played "The Star-Spangled Banner." I protested but she insisted and said I would remember this day all my life—needless to say she was right.

Lenore Boni-DiPillo

I went to the Surf Theater with my friend Nelson Axelrod. I can't recall the name of the movie, but I do remember Ilona Massey was one of the co-stars. We

walked home to Nelson's house on Maple Avenue and
someone from his family told us about the attack on
Pearl Harbor. We had no idea where Pearl Harbor
was.

Noel Schwartz

A few friends and I were at Bart Meissner's home at 3829 Beach Thirty-eighth Street that afternoon, gathered around his family's 1931 Philco 90 cathedral-style radio, listening to the New York Giants' football game.

A solemn-voiced announcer broke into the clipped cadence of the play-by-play sportscaster. *"We interrupt this program for a special bulletin. The Japanese have attacked Pearl Harbor, Hawaii, President Roosevelt has just announced."* That's when we heard the news that the Japanese bombed Pearl Harbor.

Pearl Harbor? Where was that? What did it mean? As nine-year-olds, we didn't have a clue of what kind of impact this would have on our lives. Then Bart's uncle Frank came into the room to explain that the Japanese planes had bombed the U.S. Naval base in Hawaii and this sneak attack would likely mean war for our country. Our curiosity was stirred as we realized we were present during a history-making moment on a grand scale.

Then football play resumed and all of us lost interest in listening to the news till Bart's uncle turned the dial to another station, which broadcast more of the attack in detail. We'd planned to play a round of croquet in Bart's yard later but we all stayed glued to the news. Back home, my dad had the radio on, switching back and forth to stations WEAF, WJZ, and WOR, as they all carried special reports. CBS broadcasts, however, went on as usual, airing "Burns and Allen," "Charlie McCarthy" and "Jack Benny."[15]

That evening my father and I went out the Gate to buy early editions of the *Daily News* and the *Daily Mirror.* The luncheonettes on Mermaid Avenue and West Thirty-sixth Street were closed, so we drove to an open newsstand on West Twenty-ninth, but they had sold out as soon as the bundled stack of papers hit the pavement. We headed for the stand under the El at Stillwell Avenue where we got lucky and were able to buy the morning editions. The front-page headlines were big and bold and news stories described the carnage in detail:

> *Japanese planes attacked the United States Naval Base at Pearl Harbor, Hawaii Territory, killing more than 2,300 Americans. The USS* Arizona *was completely destroyed and the USS* Oklahoma *capsized. The attack sank three other ships and damaged many additional vessels. More than 180 aircraft were destroyed.*

The next day at PS 188, Mrs. Pauline Lehman, our fourth-grade teacher, discussed the attack and the implications lying ahead for America at war. Our homework assignment for that night: to listen to President Roosevelt's broadcast and hand in a summary of his key points.

The next night, Roosevelt made an impassioned speech, and the senate unanimously endorsed his request for a Declaration of War against Japan. Three days later, Germany and Italy—fulfilling their treaty obligations with Japan—declared war against us.

Sea Gate Does Its Part

Our neighborhood wanted to support the war effort. A newsletter from the Sea Gate Association was mailed to eligible residents about the need for volunteers for the armed services, with many young local men, just one or two years out of Lincoln High School, answering the call by enlisting. As eager volunteers flooded the downtown Brooklyn Draft Board offices, ordinary citizens soon felt the impact of the war's near-term impact.

On the home front, Sea Gaters helped pay for the war's enormous cost by buying war bonds at $18.75 each. In ten years, they would be worth $25.[16] Bonds could be purchased almost immediately at the Dime Savings Bank at Mermaid Avenue and Seventeenth Street and at the Manufacturers Trust on Surf and West Twelfth. But mostly they were sold at school. At PS 188, the teachers passed out stamp books to each student, with stamps, selling for ten cents or more, pasted into our books until they added up to $18.75. And the student in each class buying the most stamps that week was given a free pass to the Surf Theater.

We were at war, and Sea Gaters reacted the way most Americans did after receiving the news: rallying in support with profound calm and a quiet determination to see it through, no matter how long it might take. All over the neighborhood, American flags flew from porches, poles, and trees. Unlike the Vietnam—and to a lesser extent, the Korean War—there was no disunity, no anti-government demonstrations, and no college sit-ins. Instead, there was a coming together of people (of all groups, classes, and countries of origin) and Japanese-Americans, in particular, into a feeling of solidarity. We were truly one nation.

Conservation

The government encouraged us to conserve and recycle materials such as metal, paper, and rubber, which factories could then reuse for wartime production—even the foil inside a pack of cigarettes or the thin wire wrapped around the lid of milk bottles. My mother would save kitchen fat and fill up tin cans to bring to a collection station near the Sea Gate office and our sanitation trucks picked up metals and rubber items on special days.

> *I recall looking for paper tin foil from abandoned cigarette packs, rolling the tin foil into a ball, and when the ball was large, submitting it towards the war effort. I recall the trucks that came around for pots and pans, also for the war effort. My family*

donated binoculars to the navy on one of their
campaigns for items to be used by our government.

Jerry Stern

I remember my friend Karl and I going from
house to house with two borrowed little red wagons
collecting old newspapers for a Scrap Paper Drive.
My father drove the papers and us to the collection
point at Mark Twain Junior High School. We collected
so much paper that it took five round trips in his
overloaded car.

Kalman Bergen

Rationing

We had just recovered from the Great Depression when we
were thrust back into another time of scarcity. Rich or poor—it
didn't matter. The playing field was leveled by the government's
Office of Price Administration (OPA), which doled out ration
cards to each family to buy such items as gasoline, coffee, sugar,
and meat. This, of course, was a frustration—not only to families,
but to merchants in the area, who had to turn away loyal customers
who requested extra butter or meat. The ban on cigarettes, a big
seller, affected even the luncheonettes in those days (and thirty-
plus years before cancer warnings); some thirty percent of all
cigarettes produced were allocated for servicemen, making packs
a scarce commodity on the home front.[17]

Weinig's Grocery store was on Twenty-ninth Street
near Mermaid Avenue. I remember going into the
store with ration stamps. Food was still rationed for
months after the war until President Truman
terminated the OPA (Office of Price Administration).
Milk was sold in bottles that were only pasteurized.
Homogenized milk was introduced a few years after
WW II. The machinery had to be designed, built and

distributed to the milk processing plants. It was a real treat not having to shake up the bottle and distribute the cream that collected on the top.

Sidney Krimsky

My father was issued a gas sticker "A"—which he pasted on his front windshield of his 1939 Oldsmobile. Since he used his car for non-essential purposes, he was restricted to three gallons a week. And, as auto plants switched to producing military vehicles, all families had to "make do" with their old models, with new car production banned (on January 1, 1942).

My friend Darryl Dworman's father, Irving, rode around during the war years in his 1938 black Plymouth coupe. Although it only was a two-seater, it was Irving's favorite. I used to wait for the trolley on Surf Avenue to visit my father in Coney Island. Irving often would stop and give me a lift when he headed for Raven Hall.

My father loved his Plymouth. He kept it several years after the war. My brothers and I bought him a new car with all the power options after the war. One day when he was driving he had the windows wide open and it started to rain. The power windows malfunctioned and he came home soaked. He thanked us for our generous gift but said, "If you don't mind boys, I'm driving my little Plymouth from now on."

Darryl Dworman

We were playing mah-jongg at Elaine Tarnapol's home on Sunday, December 7, when we learned about the Japanese attack on Pearl Harbor. I remember ration books, blackouts, air raid drills, the army encampment on the beach, the concrete foundations for anti-aircraft guns, rolling

> bandages at the Sea Gate Chapel, and not-to-be-
> forgotten, one gold star family.
>
> *Irene Needle-Halpern*

Rationing also influenced fashion. Forget about these days of the Heathers and Britneys and J. Lo's with their exposed navels. Then, "less" was more—in a patriotic sense. During the summer of '42, civilian clothing styles emphasized conserving fabric, which meant the garb for public-spirited Sea Gate women became two-piece bathing suits and shorter dresses and narrower suits. As for the men—my father couldn't buy a vest, and pants went cuff-less.

Victory Gardens

Everyone had them. For ten cents each, I bought seed packets at Woolworth's and planted a victory garden in my backyard. Perhaps I was influenced by the government's propaganda machine, but whatever the motivation, it was fun and gave me a feeling that I was doing my part for the war effort. What a tremendous feeling of satisfaction to see buds begin to sprout, and in my little ten-by-twenty-foot plot of earth. I grew radishes, corn, turnips, beets, and squash.

Posters and Flags

As more and more Sea Gate sons, brothers, husbands or fathers joined the armed forces, patriotic symbols were evident everywhere. Each family was entitled to hang a small "Son in Service" flag about one foot long, which was usually set vertically in their front window. The blue star in the center of the red-bordered white rectangle signified a family member in active service, and if a family member was killed in action, the star was replaced or covered with a gold star.

**World War II Poster. Courtesy of the National
Archives and Records Administration**

Word War II posters were displayed in the office of the Sea Gate
Association, the Sea Gate chapel, in storefronts along Mermaid Avenue,
and in banks, post offices, and schools. Branches of the armed forces,
recruiting bureaus, the Office of War Information, and the U.S. Treasury
commissioned the posters. Patriotic in nature (*i.e.*, "Uncle Sam Wants
You"), they were intended to rouse pro-American feelings, and help
mobilize citizens to support the war movement.

**World War II Poster. Courtesy of the National
Archives and Records Administration**

> *A lot of neighborhood boys went off to fight in*
> *Europe and never returned. My brothers had a friend*
> *named Stanley Greenberg, whose father owned the*
> *Baltic Linen Company—he always used to say his*
> *dad worked in a sheet house. Stanley was killed in the*
> *war. So were a lot of other boys we knew. Sea Gate is*
> *a residential community of single-family houses, and*
> *when I'd walk down the street I'd see many windows*
> *displaying the gold star.*[18]
>
> **Beverly Sills**

Blackouts

Following the attack on Pearl Harbor, Sea Gate and Coney Island residents had reason to fear an attack on their coastline from German bombing raids or the more realistic threat of German U-boats operating in the Atlantic. Ergo coastal "blackouts" and "dimouts" went into effect along a fifteen-mile strip on the Eastern Seaboard. This required that all house and streetlights along the shores be extinguished during specified curfews. In addition the headlights on cars had to be painted black on the top half of the fixture as well as the streetlights in Sea Gate.

> *I recall the large searchlights on the beach, looking*
> *for unfamiliar planes in the sky every night. The top*
> *half of all front headlights on cars were painted black*
> *so that cars at night would be more difficult to spot*
> *from the air.*
>
> **Jerry Stern**

Sea Gate's first blackout occurred at 9 P.M., March 19, 1942, and extended up twelve miles to Far Rockaway. With the bright night lit by glimmering stars and a quarter moon hanging in the western sky, residents were instructed to remain in their homes, unlighted and with all shades drawn. Air raid wardens (all civilian volunteers) manned 251 switches, and put out the 1,561 streetlights on the streets and boardwalk of Coney Island. All traffic was halted, with only wardens, police and fire officials allowed out of doors.

The blackout went off without a hitch. Mayor LaGuardia and Police Commissioner Valentine toured the area, pronounced the blackout a success. "I think that the results in the whole area were remarkably fine," Mayor LaGuardia said. "The homes responded beautifully. If everyone in the city responds as well as they did tonight everything will be all right. It was fine cooperation."[19]

Periodical blackouts were carried out over the next three months. But not everyone was happy. With summer approaching, Coney Island's amusement owners and concessionaires were concerned about their effect during the peak months of July and August, when the influx of hundreds of thousands of visitors would hit the beaches and boardwalk. To preclude the possibility of panic, an air raid warden protection service was set up to make policy and assign wardens to Brooklyn neighborhoods. Zone 1 covered Sea Gate and Coney Island, with its headquarters at the Sixtieth Precinct on West Eighth Street in Coney Island. Each amusement ride owner was to assign an employee to become an air raid warden.

Before the war, Coney Island's amusement area was aglow with a spectacle of lights that lit up the summer sky. Oliver Pilat and Jo Ranson describe the opening day glitter of Luna Park in their book, *Sodom by the Sea*:

> *When the gates opened at Luna Park, the Baghdad outline of red-and-white minarets, spires and towers were springing upward against the heavy purple sky under the illumination of 250,000 electric lights. The crowds thought Luna stood for light, just as the crowds at later Lunas in cities like London and Paris assumed that Luna stood for light. The crowds were entranced by the lighted-Christmas-tree appeal of the new Coney*

*Island Park, by its Hans Christian Andersen sort of
magic.*[20]

Luna Park (background) was lit up at night with
250,000 electric lights. It had a Baghdad
architectural-style of minarets, spires, and towers.
Photo of Arnold Rosen (in foreground) sitting on
Dad's 1931 DeSoto, circa 1933.

The larger amusement centers—such as Luna Park and
Steeplechase—had already installed central switches, which
employees could operate if an alert was sounded. And most had
night watchmen who could be instructed to darken the parks in
case of an alert signal after closing.

And as the first summer of World War II approached, Coney
Island was braced for an influx of soldiers and sailors.

The Army Lands in Sea Gate

Local preparations for war, had, indeed begun. On July 9, 1942, the U.S. Army created a unit called the "Sea Coast Fortification Battery" and stationed one hundred soldiers in prefabricated barracks on Atlantic Avenue. To protect the beachfront along the entrance of New York Harbor, the army corps of engineers erected the following facilities:

1. A seventy-foot observation tower on Atlantic Avenue and Beach Thirty-Eighth Street.
2. A camouflage-painted two-story building with a wooden roof and concrete, reinforced first floor.
3. Two concrete platforms for 90mm gun emplacements on the beach at Beach Forty-second Street.
4. Four gun platforms (for three-inch rapid fire guns) on the beach between Beach Forty-second and Beach Forty-fifth streets.
5. One platform for a searchlight on Beach Fortieth Street.

> *The army's presence on the Sea Gate beach was vivid in my memory. Once my father took me to Beach Two. He made the mistake of bringing his camera, which the Sea Gate Police confiscated, and the scene scared the hell out of me.*
>
> **Jerry Stern**

> *We lived on the second floor facing Beach Forty-fourth Street. The army placed three big anti-aircraft guns atop big cement pedestals on the beach facing out across the narrows. We were told there were nets under the water to snag any enemy submarines that might approach our shore. I used to lie in my bed, looking out the window across the ocean and wonder why I couldn't see the bombs being dropped in Europe.*

The coast guard and the army would patrol up and down the beach in front of my house and my friends and I used to talk to a Pvt. Russell Baker and Sgt. Orr every night. One night my friend, Morris Shorofsky, who lived up the block on Beach Forty-fourth Street, borrowed an officer's cap from a relative in the service and stood in the shadows on my porch, tried to make his voice deep (he was eleven years old) and told the patrol guards he was a soldier on leave. The soldier on duty played along and I still remember how we giggled and what fun we had thinking we fooled him.

Lenore Boni-DiPillo

I remember the platoon of GIs that occasionally trotted down the middle of Neptune Avenue at double time right past my house and on out to Coney Island.

Kalman Bergen

After a big snowstorm we used to take our sleds on the beach and use the big snow-covered searchlight ramp to sleigh downhill.

Harold Rosen

Harbor defense of New York was always a concern to the United States. Fort Hamilton in Brooklyn (completed in 1825) and Fort Wadsworth in Staten Island (completed in 1875) were strategically built to protect New York City from any nautical attack. During World War II, the army stretched a huge underwater net (anti-submarine nets) between the forts in order to catch enemy submarines. The nets were placed near the lagoon in the vicinity of the lighthouse. These nets were actually made of heavy chain segments hung from buoys. These were replaced by cable rings (fifteen-inch diameter) interwoven to form a length of net and were emplaced in 1942.

One configuration consisted of large floating wooden blocks

or timber anchored to the bottom, shackled together with two parallel steel cables (jackstays), which had enormous protruding star-shaped barbs.

> *Every once in a while the wooden buoys (attached to the submarine nets) would break loose and float ashore on the beach near Forty-sixth Street or on the bay side. My friends and I would discover one, remove the cotter pin, take the shackle out and carry off four or five feet of chain netting and sell it to a junkyard dealer in Coney Island.*
>
> **Noel Schwartz**

> *I remember a warm spring day in 1944, sitting on Beach Four with my friends, Florence Needle, Rhoda Eisenberg, Laurie Frankel and Anita Kaskel watching the ever-rolling sea and the water filling the lagoon formed by the rocks. Out in the ocean we thought we saw something that looked like a periscope. I went back the next day with Rhoda and we saw it again. It stayed for a while and then disappeared. We made up all kinds of scary scenarios never realizing until many years later that what we saw was for real and German U-boats had been in the waters within the area of the Narrows and along the Atlantic coast.*
>
> *We never told anyone then because we thought we were imagining the whole thing. We were only about 8 or 9 years old at the time and who would believe us. Could you imagine letting your 8 year old go to the beach with some friends alone today?*
>
> **Naomi Lipson-Hochman**

There were hundreds of German U-boat wrecks lying on the ocean floor after World War II. Five were sunk off the US Atlantic coast and one near Sea Gate.

According to Timothy Mulligan, a German Naval Historian and archivist at the National Archives and Records Administration, the positive identification of German U-boat, U-869 was discovered about 60 miles east of the New Jersey coast. This might very well be the periscope sighted by Naomi and her friends off the beach at Sea Gate. Divers and oceanographers found evidence that this U-boat was likely sunk by one of her own acoustic torpedoes.

I gave up fishing off the jetty when the war came. I gave my fishing gear to my brother, Rich, and joined the army. No one was allowed on the jetty, anyway, or on the beach for that matter. The whole place was patrolled by the military. They not only watched over the submarine net from a pillbox built just a few feet away from our front lawn, they also mounted cannons all along the beach to guard against an invasion[21]

Leonard Everett Fisher

During World War II, gun batteries were placed on the beaches and I remember that we were all warned to open our windows in advance of these 90 mm Howitzers being shot off so as to prevent breakage from the loud sounds. We all had pails of sand in our basements to help fight incendiary bombs if dropped and I trained myself in spotting enemy planes by studying plane silhouettes during nighttime. Our fathers who were in the home guard often marched on Sundays through the streets wearing civilian clothes save for the metal, debris-resistant helmets, required for them at the time.

Richard Oberfield

Concrete platform for 90 mm gun emplacements on the beach at Beach Forty-second Street. Courtesy of Charles Denson

During those winter months, we used to watch the soldiers take machine gun practice along the beach. They would launch huge balloons, taking aim at them as they rose over the Atlantic Ocean, and we could see the projectory of the tracer bullets as they were fired.

> *The billeted servicemen were often invited to neighboring homes for dinner and holiday celebrations. There were war-bond rallies to attend with our parents and the entertainment included "home town" talent Faye DeWitt and "Bubbles" Silverman (aka Beverly Sills). They were great! The sirens screamed their warnings, the searchlights fanned the skies and everyone persevered.*
>
> **Irma Freedman-Most**

> *We played softball against the U.S. Army troops every Sunday. The winning team was treated to beer after the game.*
>
> **Lenny Wachs**

At first most of the soldiers stationed in Sea Gate kept to

themselves. Then the Ladies Auxiliary of Kneses Israel, the local synagogue, sponsored a War Bond Drive at the Sea Gate Chapel and invited the soldiers to participate in festivities that night. Refreshments were served and the GIs got the chance to meet local residents. It also gave Sea Gaters a chance to thank them for their service to our country. And on June 6, 1943, in addition to the periodic open houses and invitations from Sea Gate residents for home-cooked meals, the army officially dedicated the Sea Gate Lighthouse Canteen at 4522 Beach Forty-fifth Street. The canteen, supported by the residents, provided servicemen with a mini-club with a game room, snacks, movies, and telephones to call home.

> *I was eighteen years old and a volunteer hostess at the canteen. I met this gorgeous soldier at one of the dances. His name was Roger Baker and he was married. I adored his name and vowed that I would name my first child, Roger after him—and I did.*
>
> **Pearl Hornreich**

Dedication ceremonies at the Sea Gate Canteen. Mrs. Fanny Steinberg is seated at the right and Brig. General Philip Gage of Fort Hancock, Sandy Hook, New Jersey officiated. June 6, 1943. Circa 1943. Photo courtesy of Gloria Steinberg-Gerst.

The Sea Gate Lighthouse Canteen officers: (Left to right) Mary Ziegelbaum, Emil Post, _____, Ray Greenstein, Fanny Steinberg, unidentified officer, Mary Dillon, _____, _____, Virginia Sutherland, _____. Photo, 1943 courtesy of Evalyn Greenstein-Krown

The canteen was originally planned to be run by the United Service Organization. They proposed that the Sea Gate Association provide a facility, food, entertainment, and to submit all plans to USO headquarters for approval. Joseph and Fanny Steinberg brought the proposal back to the board and the members felt that the USO proposal was too restrictive. As a result the association decided to run the canteen by themselves through volunteer service by the residents. The house was donated by Mary Elizabeth Dillon and was completely furnished with a piano, jukebox and kitchen facilities. Mrs. Ray Greenstein was in charge of buying the food. Fritzie Yampol and Ray Greenstein would arrive at 4 P.M. on weekdays to prepare sandwiches, cold cuts, coffee and cake in time for the 6 P.M. opening. On Saturdays and Sundays the canteen was open all day. Dances were planned for Saturday evenings and young single ladies of Sea Gate, such as Harriet

Harnett, Ruth Shubert, Muriel Taub and Pearl Hornreich, volunteered to be hostesses and dance partners.

The Sea Gate Association hosted a gala fund-raising luncheon at the Hotel Astor. The guest entertainer for the event was Jimmy Durante

As the war dragged on, the count rose of wounded and disabled men arriving home aboard hospital and troop ships.

> *Larry Weinberg stepped on a land mine, which was filled with shrapnel. Nobody thought he'd recover. He did survive, returned to Sea Gate after the war and eventually moved to California. He was so grateful that he survived the war that he decided to repay God for saving his life. He became one of the biggest builders of residential homes in California and owner of the Portland Trail Blazers. He has been a contributor to charitable foundations and a major donor to fund research projects in a variety of fields.*
>
> **Joel Harnett**

To make room for the incoming wounded and disabled servicemen, the U.S. Navy commissioned the Half Moon Hotel, on the boardwalk in Coney Island, as the United States Naval Convalescent Hospital, Sea Gate, Brooklyn.[22]

> *The 303-room, fifteen-story hotel, which as a beachfront hospital will have accommodations for eight hundred patients, has been undergoing extensive renovation since the navy took over on July 16. It will be ready to receive its first group of patients late in September.[23]*

On Christmas Day, 1944, the Half Moon Hotel Navy

Convalescent Hospital held an open house, with a concert and movies plus plenty of assistance from Sea Gate's volunteers. And throughout the holiday, the volunteers continued to help, donating candy, cigarettes, playing cards, and shaving supplies—and especially their time.

Prior to the Christmas open house the Sea Gate Lighthouse Canteen sponsored several dances at the naval hospital. The navy expressed their gratitude to the Sea Gate volunteers for their service in a letter.

U.S. NAVAL CONVALESCENT HOSPITAL
Sea Gate, Brooklyn 24, New York

17 November 1944

Sea Gate Lighthouse Canteen
Sea Gate
Brooklyn, New York

Dear Junior and Senior Hostesses:

We're really at a loss for words here at the hospital today. Perhaps the one word "Wonderful" would be appropriate. Our dancing partners were wonderful, our chaperones were wonderful, the refreshments were wonderful and all together made a wonderful dance.

It was very nice of you to come to our dance and thus insure its success. May I thank you on behalf of the medical officer in command, the men of the hospital and my personnel thanks for all you did for us.

Sincerely yours,

R. KORSGAARD
Lt. (jg) USNR
Welfare and Recreation Officer

I remember the Half Moon Hotel was used as a naval hospital during WW II and the wounded sailors would be wheeled out on the boardwalk for some fresh air. My father and mother went there for their honeymoon in 1935, when it was an exclusive hotel. It was the tallest building in Coney Island and visible for miles around. I remember, as a kid, just walking into the lobby and looking around without anyone suspecting me of anything except curiosity. Now, there are turnstiles that require a plastic card and swipe reader. Everything is focused on security these days.

Sid Krimsky

I was wounded in France in World War II and I was sent to a general hospital near Devizes, England. As I was being wheeled into the room on a gurney, the ward doctor asked me about my hometown. When I told him that I was from Sea Gate he said that there was another wounded soldier in the ward from there. I went over to him and met Hy Ochacher for the first time even though he and his family lived only a few blocks away. I knew the family name, but as Hy was about eight or nine years my senior, I had never met him. We both had similar wounds and we both had surgery within a short while of each other. We became friends during our extended stay and saw each other after the war.

Al Goldstein

Stanley Greenberg, Stanley Gladstone and Joe Pearl, among

many other Sea Gaters, made the ultimate sacrifice during World War II. The English erected a monument in memory of airmen who were killed in World War II. Stanley Greenberg's name was inscribed on this memorial edifice.

World War II Ends

> There'll be bluebirds over the white cliffs of Dover tomorrow, just you wait and see.
> There'll be love and laughter and peace ever after tomorrow, when the world is free.[24]

Everyone in America waited for the words of this song (most popularly sung by Kate Smith) to become a reality. Finally, on May 7, 1945, VE Day (Victory in Europe) arrived, the day of Germany's surrender, officially ending the European phase of World War II.

V-J Day (Victory over Japan) was to follow on August 15, with Emperor Hirohito formally signing Japan's surrender on September 2. Peace at last.

Let the Celebrations Begin

Though I vividly recall the December 7 Japanese attack on Pearl Harbor, it's not so for VE or VJ Day. Still, vague memories remain—of listening to the radio broadcasts describing the celebration in Times Square, reading about it in the *Daily News* and *Life* magazine, and watching the Fox and Movietone News clips at the Saturday matinee in the Surf Theater.

> I remember the day when the war ended. My mother's friend, Henny Brenner (mother of Donald, Philip, and Gloria), heard the commotion on the street where she lived on Lyme Avenue. People were outside yelling, "The war is over, the war is over!" She came out of her house wearing a nightgown and robe and

*smoking a cigarette. In her excitement the cigarette
accidentally ignited her bathrobe and she was very
badly burnt.*

Barbara Harnett-Weil

*I remember the block parties after the war. Lou
Stillman created wonderful shows on Cypress Avenue.
We all sang and danced and wore costumes and had
the best of times. Growing up in Sea Gate was magical!*

Carole Mennen-Gabay

Welcome Home. A Job Well Done

"**Welcome Home—Well Done**" In large bold letters, and
visible as you rode past it on the Belt Parkway, this was the sign
erected on a sloping grassy knoll outside the perimeter of
Brooklyn's Fort Hamilton. But mainly, it was intended to be
seen by the returning war vets steaming into New York Harbor
on troop ships. Welcoming signs were also displayed on the
homes in Sea Gate, from Surf Avenue to the houses on the bay
along Ocean View Avenue.

And Sea Gate's returning vets wasted no time getting back to
civilian life—after all, they had to catch up on the years spent
overseas, from the battlefields of Guadalcanal and New Guinea
to North Africa and Salerno. So they enrolled in college under
the GI Bill, or resumed their old jobs, or for the moment, just
relaxed and enjoyed the hospitality of friends and family. And
peace.

Night out at the Glen Island Casino in New Rochelle from left to right: Alvin Dworman, Barbara Harnett, Sandy Levine, (unidentified), Seymour "Jeep" Lefkowitz, Norma Tonkin, (unidentified), Sandy "Wacky" Levitt.

In 1946, a group of Sea Gate veterans formed the **A.V. Sea Gate**, a branch of the American Veterans Committee, and published a newsletter of the same name, devoted to social and political issues affecting local life. Committee members included Paul Hessel, chairman; Joe Muldavin, editor; and Murray Benson, associate editor, who also wrote a regular column, "Peekin' Thru the Gate." Membership quickly grew to 220 the first year, and the Women's Auxiliary AVC to fifty.

Cultural Life: Sea Gate's returning servicemen took a major role in activities at the Sea Gate center, part of the Congregation Kneses Israel. Centrally located at the corner of Nautilus and Sea Gate Avenues, it provided prayer, forums, and dances not only for the veterans but for other residents as well. Bill Suffin, Abe Plattman, Harry Greenstein, and Rabbi Ezra Gellman were all instrumental in the center's success, contributing to a rich and wholesome cultural outlet for the area.

Sports: No more war games. Softball was the sport of choice, which the vets loved to play. Early weekend mornings found gatherings for "choose-up" teams at the Sea Gate tennis courts.[25]

Enthusiasm for softball heightened in the spring of 1946 as vets, combined with other residents, began to form teams for a league. Stands and a scoreboard were erected, and an "all-star" Sea Gate team was selected to compete with other Brooklyn softball teams. The manager was George Sommer and some of the players included Ray Shore, Sandy Levine, Howie and Monnie Adler, Walter Wagman, Irv Plattman, Murray Zuckerman, Jerry Leibowitz, Irv "Cooney" Reiss, Sandy "Wacky" Levitt, Harry Rattner, Irv Schreiber, Lenny Wachs, and Joe Frank.

Lenny Wachs leaps for a high one

Swinging for the fences. Ronnie Berliner at bat in a softball game at Sea Gate tennis court. Freeze-frame photo from old 8mm home movie by Arnold Rosen. Circa 1948

The remnants of World War II remained in Sea
Gate for several years after the war. Pictured in
the background, was the US Army seventy-foot-
tall observation tower as we played basketball at
the Riviera. Freeze-frame photo from 8mm home
movie by Arnold Rosen circa 1949.

CHAPTER 7

STORMS OVER SEA GATE

The Perils of Mother Nature

Snowstorms, hurricanes, coastal flooding, and torrential rains have inundated Sea Gate's hardy residents for more than a hundred years. The geography of this fenced community on the western tip of Coney Island that juts out into the Atlantic can make for an idyllic haven or a curse. Residents face ongoing battles to save their waterfront homes from the sometimes thundering Atlantic Ocean. The effects of storms are especially devastating to residents along Atlantic and Ocean View avenues, and the Beach Streets. In its wake, storms can leave a trail of battered homes, lost windows, porches and walls. Basements and more can be flooded, and clothes, furnishings, and other property are vulnerable to heavy damage. Despite these ravages homeowners repair, regroup, and brace themselves for the next assault from Mother Nature.

Types of Storms

Nor'easters: These weather events are among winter's most ferocious storms. The name is derived from its continuously strong northeasterly winds blowing in from the ocean ahead of the storm and over coastal areas. Nor'easters are notorious for producing heavy rain, snow, and oversized waves that crash onto the beaches of Sea Gate, often causing beach erosion and structural damage. Wind gusts associated with these storms can exceed hurricane force intensity. These strong areas of low pressure often form either in the Gulf of Mexico or off the East Coast in the Atlantic Ocean. The low will then either move up the East Coast into New England, the Atlantic provinces of Canada or veer off out to sea.

Hurricanes and Cyclones: Storm surge, high winds, heavy rain, and flooding are the main hazards associated with hurricanes and cyclones. A storm surge is a large dome of water, fifty to one hundred miles wide, that sweeps across the coastline near where a hurricane makes landfall. These storms can be especially devastating to Sea Gate residents along the beach line as the surge of high water topped by waves can be the greatest threat to life and property. Hurricane winds usually accompany storm surges. The intensity of the winds not only damage structures, but the fallout of airborne debris can be dangerous to anyone unfortunate to be caught out on the streets. Tropical cyclones originate in the south, but they can also migrate northward toward Sea Gate. These storms frequently produce huge amounts of rain, and flooding, particularly for residents along the beaches. A sudden deluge of six to twelve inches of rain can result in considerable home damage and in extreme cases, injury and loss of life.

For the elderly residents of Sea Gate, these hazards can bring other consequences not directly related to the storm. For example, heart attacks as a result of shoveling snow during the cleanup phase and fires started by candles used when the electricity fails.

Historic Sea Gate Storms

The Blizzard of '47: On December 27, 1947, a major snowstorm hit New York City. Approximately twenty-six inches of snow fell in the region and Sea Gate had drifts up to twenty-nine inches. Nobody was prepared for a storm this bad. Weather forecasting at the time was not as sophisticated as it is today. The blizzard was caused by a strong upper air disturbance and copious amounts of moisture. It became the worst snowstorm in the city's history, surpassing the snowfall totals from the blizzard of 1888, which had a total of approximately twenty-two inches of the white stuff.

The Blizzard of 1947. Four days after, Harold Rosen sleds down Surf Avenue.

In Sea Gate, cars were buried in snow. Buses were useless and the tracks on Norton's Point trolley were buried.[26] The Gate's sanitation trucks were finally dug out after three days. Plows were attached and the trucks lumbered through the streets providing a narrow path for buses and cars. Schools were closed for the Christmas break and kids were experiencing "cabin fever" after being confined for two to three days. Young children romped in the snow, built snowmen, igloos, and bellywhapped on their Flexible Flyer sleds on the streets. Daring older teens—as Lenny

Wachs and others report in this book—attached sleds to the rear of the buses by looping a rope around the rear bumper of the Sea Gate bus. "Daredevils" riders flew around the Gate, on the sled in the snow, choking and laughing as they breathed the black fumes from the bus exhaust.[27]

I remember the blizzard of '47. I went with my boyfriend to Madison Square Garden to see José Gonzales play a tennis match. When we got outside, the snow just started to fall and soon it was up to our waists.

Martha Goldstein-Reinken

I had a Flexible Flyer sled. What fun I had being towed behind a car on my sled through the snow-covered streets in Sea Gate. Heavy snowfalls would usually isolate Sea Gate from the rest of Brooklyn and made the streets impassable. My father was in the fuel oil business and dispatched a truck to Sea Gate to help his neighbors. The driver was unfamiliar with the streets, so Don Brenner's father climbed aboard the truck to direct the driver.

Irma Freedman-Most

It seemed to snow more in the 1930s. I remember waking up one morning to see Myron Buchman, wearing his fur hat, ice-skating all alone in the middle of Surf Avenue. I also remember snowball fights with Coney Island kids with missiles flying over the fence separating the two communities—an annual ritual every winter.

Joel Harnett

I remember the blizzard of 1947 when I went to my uncle's wedding and had to be carried from Mermaid Avenue to our home at 3782 Surf Avenue because the snow was so deep we had to leave the car outside the Sea Gate fence.

Eugene Martin (Eugene lived next to us on Surf Avenue and was a good friend of my younger brother, Harold. He had polio when he was a child and had to wear braces.)

Hurricane Donna: Hurricane Donna was born in the northeast Caribbean late on September 4, 1960, gaining speed as it raced northward toward the United States. It rampaged across Puerto Rico and the Bahamas before swiping southern Florida on September 10 with 135-mph sustained winds and peak gusts to 175 mph in the Florida Everglades. Donna then turned tail and, crossing the Florida peninsula, raced northward along the East Coast, lashing every state from South Carolina to New York with hurricane-force winds. Residents of Sea Gate heard the forecast of Donna on the radio and began taking precautions by boarding up their windows on beachfront homes, stocking up on water and candles; some even began to evacuate. Hardware stores along Mermaid Avenue soon ran out of batteries, and Tom Tesauro's lumber yard on Cropsey Avenue in Coney Island did a brisk business in plywood.

On September 12, Donna hit Sea Gate with wind gusts of one hundred miles an hour. Sea Gaters survived with some trees being uprooted and beachfront bulkheads damaged. No residents were hurt.

Hurricane Gloria: Hurricane Gloria was the seventh storm of the 1985 season, and was by far the strongest in the Atlantic. The storm began as a tropical depression far in the Eastern Atlantic on September 16 and began moving to the west-northwest over the next several days. As Gloria continued to head toward the Eastern U.S. coastline, the storm steadily weakened. Brushing North Carolina's outer islands near midnight on September 27, the winds had dropped to 105 mph. Ten hours later, the eye of the storm crossed Long Island, Coney Island, and Sea Gate with winds of seventy mph.

It slammed into the Gate with pounding winds and heavy rains, though most of the region appeared to take the awesome storm in stride.

With thousands of people staying home from jobs and school, commuter trains rode half empty, road traffic was light and pedestrians on rain-soaked city streets were sparse. Residents of Sea Gate, Brighton Beach, and Coney Island were taken to several shelters in South Brooklyn after the police drove through the streets with loudspeakers urging them to leave.

The Halloween Storm of 1991: The National Weather Service also labeled this nor'easter "**The Perfect Storm.**" Mariners bore most of the brunt of this fierce oceanic storm, which resulted in the sinking of the fishing boat *Andrea Gail*, whose story became the basis for the best-selling novel, *The Perfect Storm* by Sebastian Junger, as well as the movie starring George Clooney.

On October 30, the storm began to move slowly up the east coast, creating ferocious waves up and down the entire Eastern Seaboard. It swept away chunks of the Jersey shoreline, and moved into southern New England with a vengeance. It battered Sea Gate and Long Island with its high winds, pounding waves and tidal flooding.

Hundreds of residents of Sea Gate worked through the night of the storm to pile thousands of twenty-five-pound sandbags in place of a concrete bulkhead that collapsed at the foot of Beach Forty-fourth Street. The bulkhead, a man-made patchwork of steel, timber, and reinforced concrete ran three thousand feet, hugging the shore properties. It was built to protect beachfront homeowners against the ocean's fury. But this barrier was no match for the gale force winds and towering waves. The bulkhead gave way around 2:30 A.M., leaving a fifty-foot break through which torrents of seawater poured. Some residents of the street were evacuated but all returned the next morning to survey the damage. Damage was confined mostly to porches and decks behind the homes, but much of the beach had vanished.

Lasting only five days, **the Perfect Halloween Storm of 1991** has been considered the most extreme nor'easter since 1932. With seventy mph wind gusts and fifteen-foot waves crashing onshore, this storm eroded over a thousand miles of coastline along the East Coast.

Three-Day Nor'easter (December 10, 11, 12, 1992): Residents in Sea Gate, still struggling to recover from the flooding of a vicious storm and high tides the previous December, began battening down for yet another assault from the sea. During the three-day storm, Sea Gate endured a total of seven high tides—the normal high tide occurs every twelve hours. Homeowners and renters alike watched in awe as an angry sea once again lashed at their homes, toppling one and threatening several more along the beachfront. In a dramatic video sequence, TV viewers watched in horror as a waterfront house owned by ophthalmologist Dr. Cohen at 4401 Beach Forty-fourth Street collapsed like a deck of cards and was devoured by the raging sea. Fortunately the house had been abandoned during the storm and no casualties occurred. Pete Spanakos, in charge of storm control, accidentally fell down a water sewer. "Some of my neighbors were afraid I would reenter in one of their toilets," he joked. "Anyway, the cops and firemen pulled me up and out of the sewer."

It was a day of heavy snow and dreary gloom across much of Brooklyn and Long Island's shoreline. Sea Gate together with homes along the Jersey and Long Island coast suffered devastating losses. There were thousands of battered homes, lost windows, porches and walls; basements and whole houses were flooded, and clothes, furnishings, lawns, fences, and other property were heavily damaged. The cabana complex and Riviera on Beach One was in a state of utter devastation; the cabanas, as well as the showers, were destroyed. Concrete decks shattered and the Riviera restaurant was littered with debris. The two swimming pools were on the verge of collapse. Con Ed workers responded to power failures and insurance agents roamed the streets assessing damage. The police cordoned off sections flooded by the high tides. People empted their flooded basements with buckets and electric pumps. Claire Horman, a 51-year-old, who lived in a studio apartment near Atlantic Avenue, decided to evacuate after seeing the water rising all around her building. She and about forty other evacuees trudged up the watery streets and took temporary residence at the Abraham Residence, a home for the elderly on Surf Avenue. Later in that day, Mayor Dinkins visited to see how the evacuees were being treated. Mrs. Horman walked up to the mayor and expressed appreciation and thanked him for his concern. "I've been through two storms before," said Mrs. Horman, "but this is the worst. I feel strange. I feel lost. And I just want to get on with my life." Mayor Dinkins told the Sea Gaters that the three shore communities hit hardest by the storm were Broad Channel, Queens, almost all of the one thousand homes and bungalows were severely damaged by wind or flooding; **Sea Gate** where scores of homes were flooded and damaged; and Edgewater Park, the Bronx, where a seawall was breached. Governor Mario Cuomo asked the National Guard to help in the cleanup at Sea Gate.

Other Nor'easters

March 13, 1993: With wind gusts of ninety miles an hour and blowing snows, a blizzard struck the New York region and buried Sea Gate under "white-out" conditions. Residents of the Gate coped with the growing anxiety that basic utility services and food supplies would be sharply crimped before the storm was finished. Those that prepared for the storm before it hit had stocked up on basic necessities. Others who trudged out of the Gate during the storm to "mom and pop" delis to buy a quart of milk and a loaf of bread were out of luck. Supermarkets on Neptune Avenue and surrounding small stores had suffered the greatest crush of panic buying on Friday, as forecasts of the storm stirred tenants out of the Coney Island project housing complexes to buy candles, batteries, bread, canned goods and bottled water.

The outdoor concerns of the storm ranged from mundane snow shoveling to more frantic labors by Sea Gate residents. My friend, ex-neighbor, and Boy Scoutmaster (when I lived in Sea Gate), Stanley Ferber, was busy shoveling snow in front of his house at 3848 Atlantic Avenue.[28] Always the optimist, Stanley assured his worried neighbor and friend, Barbara Behar, that "Everything will be okay, and this too shall pass."

December 11, 1993: Another three-day storm hit Sea Gate and the New York region on a Friday. It was one of the most powerful nor'easters to strike the region in thirty years. Once again, shorefront homes along Sea Gate's Atlantic Avenue were damaged by high tides that rampaged over bulkheads and sea walls.

Although much has been done since the Perfect Storm (aka the Halloween Storm) to restore beaches and buildings, Sea Gate residents still feel vulnerable to the storms of the future. The beaches of Sea Gate were so badly scoured by erosion the previous December (see narrative above) that many areas lay exposed to lesser winter storms. Not only were homeowners along Sea Gate's oceanfront fearful of floodwaters that future storms would bring, (and still are) but also Sea Gate's inland residents of Laurel, Cypress, Maple, and Nautilus Avenues. Many Sea Gate homeowners have not been covered by insurance and did not qualify for assistance programs. The costs of getting back on their feet came out of their pocket.

In 1993 the United States Army Corps of Engineers started beach replenishment projects by pumping sand along a 3.5-mile stretch of Coney Island, as well as working on an 850-foot seawall to protect the beach and low-lying community within Sea Gate.

February 17, 2003 (The President's Day Storm): The worst blizzard in seven years not only socked the city in chest-high drifts of snow, but also wiped away what little was left of the beach in Sea Gate (see below). Some hardy souls took to the streets in skis along Surf and Atlantic Avenues while other young entrepreneurs went house to house offering their snow-removal services to elderly homeowners. Roads were impassable throughout the five boroughs, stranding travelers as train, plane and bus service ground to a halt in many places. Airports experienced widespread cancellations and massive delays. LaGuardia Airport closed all its runways at midmorning. Almost all domestic flights into and out of John F. Kennedy Airport were scrapped.

Barbara Brown-Cramer was scheduled to fly from JFK Airport to Ft. Lauderdale to attend the 2003 Sea Gate Reunion in Boca Raton, Florida. Her flight was rescheduled for the following day; she managed to arrive at the luncheon just in time for the first course.

Sea Gaters took the brunt of the storm in stride but this time, the storm took a big bite out of the beach. "The level of sand is as low as it's ever been, and if it gets any worse, homes are going to be threatened," warned Pete Spanakos, the resident historian. I visited Sea Gate on Thursday, February 20, three days after the storm, for a scheduled interview with Bruce Akrongold and Sal Argano of the Sea Gate Beach Club. They were surveying the storm's damage to the club and the homes along the shore. "This blizzard wasn't the first big storm we've had," Argano said. "We got hit hard with an earlier storm, and we took another shellacking this week."

The thirty homeowners along the ocean are fearful of the next storm to hit. They are hopeful that replenishing the beach to combat further erosion will take place soon. Sal and Bruce had to leave for another meeting; I had the opportunity to stroll on the beach for the first time in fifty years. It was a beautiful, sunny, cloudless day as I made my way down from the Beach One gate onto the sand. I passed three workers putting up fencing on the beach to prevent any further loss of sand. They stopped work long enough to pose for a photo. I gazed at the ocean.

Workers putting up fencing along Beach One in
Sea Gate to limit loss of sand. Photo by Arnold
Rosen, 2/20/03.

The rocks were glistening in the sun and further out on the
ocean a tanker passed into view. I approached the jetty that
separated Beach One from Beach Two and remembered a photo
that my cousin Hank and I posed for with his life raft on that
spot almost sixty years ago. At that time the beaches were 200 to
300 feet wide.

Arnold Rosen and his cousin, Hank Marcus, on
Beach Two, circa 1945.

Erosion took its toll on beaches and at some points the
beaches were reduced to a mere fifteen feet.

CHAPTER 8

PROFILES

Notable Residents of Sea Gate

Notable Sea Gate residents—full and part time—have included New York Governor Al Smith, opera diva Beverly Sills, actress Sarah Bernhardt, and Nobel Prize laureate Isaac Bashevis Singer.[29] The path honoring Sea Gate-born or based notables over the years ranges from Dr. Martin Couney and groundbreaking executive Mary Elizabeth Dillon to such as songwriter Kadish Millet, Hollywood producer Marvin Minoff, and real estate magnate Alfred Kaskel.

That Sea Gate would spawn or harbor so many illustrious residents can be ascribed in part to the beauty of a seaside resort, with its expansive beaches and breathtaking views over bay and ocean that provide a magnificent marine panorama. Against the stress of the ever-burgeoning commerce and competition of Manhattan, Sea Gate has offered aspiring entrepreneurs, scientists, writers, and artists a greater measure of fortifying elements of splendor, tranquility, privacy, and safety.

Dr. Martin Couney

Dr. Couney was a pediatrician who developed incubators for premature babies. He exhibited the "premies" in Luna Park and the 1930 World's Fair. During that time, of 8,500 premature babies, he saved 7,500, a record unmatched throughout the world. An Alsatian born in Germany, he began to specialize in pediatrics at a Parisian hospital in the early 1890s. Premature babies were left to die in those days, or were placed under blankets, surrounded by hot bricks, on a kitchen stove, a primitive method that usually did not provide the moisture necessary for survival.

Dr. Couney exhibited undersized babies at twenty-three world's fairs, ranging in location from Rio de Janeiro to Moscow. His success at two American expositions led Frederic Thompson (Thompson and Elmer Dundy were the original owners and operators of Luna Park) to suggest in 1933 that the incubators be moved to Coney Island, the capital of the amusement world. The building in Coney Island was made into a replica of a miniature hospital. Visitors were able to view the babies as they dozed in the incubators. Occasionally the nurses would wrap them in blankets, pick them up and carry them closer to the sealed windows of the room so that visitors had a better view. A lecturer explained the incubators in details. The oxygen brought in by the tube enabled the baby's lungs to function properly and avoid bronchial troubles and pneumonia. Hot water pipes connected with a boiler and regulated by a thermostat provided extra heat. An electric motor from an outside pipe went through a triple filter system for the removal of other impurities and provided pure air for the room. A small suction fan in a glass chimney atop each incubator, provided a complete change of atmosphere every five seconds.

At the 1933-34 World's Fair in Chicago, where a million and a quarter people visited the baby incubators, Dr. Couney had four prematures at one time weighing less than two pounds, all of whom left their beds in good condition. The smallest baby handled by him at Coney Island weighed a pound and a half, a quarter of a pound heavier than the smallest surviving baby recorded in medical literature.

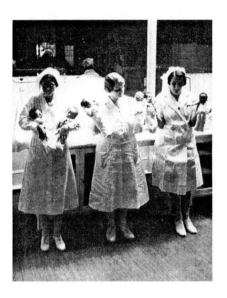

Nurses holding premature babies at Coney Island, 1939. Each baby averages two pounds. Photo: Fred, Hess & Company

Dr. Couney's home at 3726 Surf Avenue in Sea Gate. Photo by Arnold Rosen

Dr. Couney lived in Sea Gate at 3726 Surf Avenue for fifty

years until his death on March 1, 1950.

Governor Al Smith (1873-1932)

Sea Gate was the place where New York's Governor Al Smith spent many summers, especially when he was in the mood for a dip in the ocean. The governor's mother and his sister, Mrs. John Glynn, owned a home in the Gate. Al Smith was born in New York City. After a brief formal education, he worked at the Fulton Fish Market, became a member of the Democratic Party and in 1903 was elected to the state assembly.

Elected governor of New York for four terms (1919-20, 1923-28), Smith sought to end child labor and improve factory laws, housing and the care of the mentally ill. In 1928, Franklin D. Roosevelt urged him to run for the presidency. Political observers believed that his religion—Catholicism—combined with his opposition to Prohibition led to his defeat by Republican Herbert Hoover.

He became close friends with Roosevelt and supported him for president in 1932.

Beverly Sills

Beverly Sills lived in Sea Gate during the war years of 1941 to 1945. She once wrote, "Our safe little haven was turned upside down during the war years. Our house was right on the ocean and we'd see troop ships leaving for Europe every day."

She was born Belle Miriam Silverman on May 25, 1929, in Brooklyn to Shirley and Morris Silverman, of Russian-Jewish descent. She spent the first ten years of her life on Empire Street in Crown Heights. When she was three years old, she won a beautiful baby contest singing, "The Wedding of Jack and Jill." Her mother was convinced of her musical talents and provided her with lessons in dance, voice, and elocution. She launched her professional career on radio WOR (Uncle Bob's Rainbow House) in 1936 and in the 1938 film, *Uncle Sol Solves It*. She appeared in a national touring company of Gilbert and Sullivan and in 1955 became a member of the New York City Opera starring as Rosalinde in Johann Strauss's *Die Fledermaus.*

Beverly Sills.

Many years ago our family vacationed in Tanglewood, Massachusetts. Seated at our dining room table was Beverly Sill's mother. She became friendly with us after knowing that we both lived in Sea Gate. She told us that she was good friends with Mrs. Radetsky. "See this bracelet I am wearing?" she asked. "This bracelet was given to Beverly for her sixteenth birthday by Sandy Levine."

Evalyn-Greenstein-Krown

"Bubbles" Silverman used to wait with us for the bus to take us to Mark Twain Junior High School. I remember her as a very vivacious and outgoing gal with a warm and friendly smile.

Martha Goldstein-Reinken

Isaac Bashevis Singer (1904-1988)

Isaac Bashevis Singer was born in Poland to parents who were religious Jews. They pushed him towards a career as a religious scholar. In Warsaw his father supervised a *beth din*, or rabbinical court. In 1921 he enrolled in a rabbinical school, but left only two years later to work for *Literarische Bleter*, a Yiddish literary magazine as a proofreader. By 1932 he had published his first book, *Satin in Goray.*

In 1935 Singer joined the staff of the *Jewish Daily Forward* as foreign correspondent. To flee from anti-Semitism, he moved that year to the United States, parting from his first wife, Rachel, and son, Israel, who went to Moscow and later, Palestine. Singer settled in New York, where he worked for the *Forward.* He moved to Brooklyn and stayed in Sea Gate (at 4200 Atlantic Avenue) for extended visits to write and enjoy its tranquil setting and its easy accessibility to other parts of Brooklyn and Manhattan. Singer wrote:

> *We came to Coney Island. To the left, the ocean flashed and flared with a blend of water. To the right, carrousels whirled, youths shot at tin ducks. We drove through a gate with a barrier and guarded by a policeman, and it suddenly grew quiet and pastoral. We pulled up before a house with turrets and a long porch where elderly people sat and warmed themselves in the sun. My brother said, "This is the bastion of Yiddishism. Here, it's decided who is mortal or immortal, who is progressive or reactionary."[30]*

Before he moved to Atlantic Avenue, Isaac stayed with his older brother (IJ) on Beach Forty-sixth Street. It was a small room lit only by a ceiling lamp. The furnishings were scant— besides the bed there was a dresser and a bookcase containing Israel Joshua's Yiddish books. There was a bathroom in the hall, which he shared with his brother's family. On the first night he became restless and decided to take a walk by himself. Singer describes how he felt that night:

> *I trembled about getting lost in such a tiny community as Sea Gate. I had walked not knowing where, and had to come to the beach. This wasn't the open sea, since I could see lights flashing on some faraway shore. A lighthouse cast its beams. The foamy waves mounted and crashed against a stony breakwater. The beach wasn't sandy but overgrown with weeds. Chunks of driftwood and vegetation spewed forth by the sea. I trod on seashells. I picked one up and studied it—the armor of the creature that had been born in the sea and apparently had died there as well, or had been eaten despite its protection.*[31]

During the 1940s Singer published his work in a number of journals as well as serially in the *Forward*. By the 1970s, he had become a major international writer; dozens of his stories were eventually collected into books, and published in Yiddish, English and many other languages worldwide. In 1974 he won the Noble Prize in literature; in 1988 he died in Surfside, Florida.

Older brother IJ was also an author (and playwright). His epic masterpiece, *The Brothers Ashkenazy*, dated to 1936. He emigrated to the United States in 1934, and rented an apartment from the Shorofsky family at 4406 Beach Forty-fourth Street in Sea Gate.

Dr. Paul Berg

Paul Berg moved to Sea Gate in the summer of 1937, living for a while on Surf Avenue then moved to Laurel Avenue. He attended PS 188, Mark Twain Junior High School, and graduated from Lincoln High School in 1943. After one semester at Brooklyn College, he and Gene Rifkin enlisted in the navy air corps and both were sent to Penn State University to wait for call-up orders.

He received a BS in biochemistry from Penn State University and a Ph.D. from Western Reserve University in 1952.

Paul Berg in Sea Gate wearing Oriole sweater

In Lincoln High School, he came under the spell of an inspiring teacher, Sophie Wolfe. While her job was to supervise the stockroom that supplied the classes in chemistry, physics and biology, her love of young people led her to start an after-school program of science clubs. She had a special talent for drawing students out. Berg remembers the many hours after classes finished, when he worked in her laboratory. "She never gave answers to questions we asked; instead she encouraged us to find out for ourselves. Sometimes that meant doing an experiment, sometimes it meant going to the library, but it was always we who had to solve the problem." The satisfaction derived from solving a problem with an experiment was a very heady experience. Looking back, Berg feels developing curiosity and the instinct for seeking creative solutions are perhaps the most important contributions education can make. "With time," he says, "many facts we are asked to learn will be forgotten but we are less likely to lose our ability to question and discover."

Paul Berg witnessed firsthand the history of recombinant DNA research and regulation, having been in the forefront of both movements since he was a young man. He became a professor of biochemistry at Stanford University School of Medicine in 1959, when he was thirty-three. He was elected to the National Academy of Sciences before he was forty, and gained early recognition and influence when he delineated the key steps in which DNA produces proteins. Berg was awarded the Nobel Prize for chemistry in 1980 for his work with DNA.

His fond memories of Sea Gate follows:

> *My closest friends during my Sea Gate days were Gene Rifkin, Stanley Greenberg (killed in France 1944-45), Stanley Katz, and Jerry Daniels. There were others who were part of the crowd: SandyLevine, Sandy Levitt, Richie Ehrman, and Buddy Benjamin. "Bubbles" Silverman (Beverly Sills) lived close by and was part of the crowd except she was often away with her singing lessons and attendance at Erasmus High School. My girlfriends were Gloria Harnick and Barbara Harnett and although, at the time, we were rather intense, neither lasted the separation of going off to university and the service.*
>
> *The Oriole football team included many of my friends and we played "club" football with other local teams on the "tennis courts." Baseball was played near the pier and basketball, on the street.*
>
> *Sea Gate was an ideal setting for the pre and teen years. There were close friends, the freedom to come and go as we wanted and in complete safety.*

There were the usual high jinks that got us in trouble,
but by and large, it was a happy experience.

Paul Berg (extreme right) on leave from the Navy
with Sea Gate friends posing at a Coney Island
photo gallery (from left to right) Gene Rifkin,
Stanley Greenberg, and Stanley Katz. Their dear
friend, Stanley Greenberg, was killed in Europe a
day or two before VE Day. Photo courtesy of Gene
Rifkin, 1944.

The photo above struck a chord. I knew them all.
In fact I saw Gene Rifkin some ten years ago when I
did a program in Florida. The photo of Stanley
Greenberg drove me to tears. I knew his entire family.
I may have been the last Sea Gater to see him alive. It
was November 1944 at Camp Miles Standish,
Peabody, Massachusetts. I was in the first U.S. Army
group to be reassigned from the European-
Mediterranean Theater of operations to the Pacific. I
landed in Boston and was on my way home for a
nineteen-day rest. As my group was waiting to be
billeted, I spotted Stanley marching off to a train that
would take him to the ship that would soon land him

in France. I chatted with him for a couple of minutes.
A year before this, November 24, 1943, I passed Sam
Nelkin (another Sea Gater and Lincoln HS classmate)
as we were boarding the same ship in Norfolk,
Virginia. We landed in Casablanca, French Morocco.
Sam survived the war.

Leonard Everett Fisher

Leonard Everett Fisher

Bronx (New York) born (1924) and Sea Gate bred, Leonard Everett Fisher lived at 4810 Beach Forty-eighth Street. A World War II veteran, Leonard served (1942-1946) at home and overseas with the U.S. Army Corps of Engineers, creating operational maps for Mediterranean-European and Pacific invasions and battles. Following the war, he graduated from Yale University's School of Art with BFA and MFA degrees, winning the John Fergurson Weir Prize and a Winchester Traveling Fellowship.

His art can be seen in collections nationwide, including those of the Butler Art Institute, Mt. Holyoke College, the Library of Congress, the Smithsonian Institution, the New York and Westport libraries, the New Britain Museum of American Art, the Housatonic Museum, Brown University, and the Museum of American Illustration.

In a publishing career spanning forty-nine years, he has illustrated some 260 books for young readers, authoring eighty-nine of these. Among them are two Sea Gate-inspired books— *Sky, Sea, and Me* and *The Jetty Chronicles*. The latter describes the adventures of a boy growing up in the 1930s in Sea Gate filled with colorful characters. In addition he has designed United States postage stamps including *The Legend of Sleepy Hollow* and eight bicentennial commemoratives.

In 1998, the University of Connecticut, which maintains a significant archive of his books, papers and art at the Thomas J. Dodd Research Center (Storrs), published a full-color monograph,

Leonard Everett Fisher: A Life of Art, in recognition of his long career and body of work. He is married to the former Margery Meskin, a retired school librarian; they are parents of three children and grandparents of six.

Leonard Everett Fisher debarking San Francisco, CA (from USS Isaac Mayer Wise) from Ft. Kamehameha, Hawaii and sent to MacDowell Air Force Base to fly to Ft. Dix, New Jersey to be discharged, January 22, 1946

One historic incident that has stuck was seeing the German airship Hindenburg pass over the rock-strewn baseball field at the yacht club site off Poplar Avenue while we were playing a pick-up game. It was a drizzly late afternoon in May 1937. The ship seemed to fishtail as it came out of the mist from Manhattan and turned to cross the Lower Bay on its way to Lakehurst, New Jersey, about thirty-five to forty miles as the crow flew from where we stood. The Hindenberg was flying very low. We could see people waving at us from the forward cabin. When we saw the Nazi swastika on its tail we began throwing rocks at the huge ship. The ship was too high to strike, but we 13-year-olds had terrific arms. A couple of hours later we found out that the ship had exploded.

My own life in Sea Gate ended to all practical purposes when I left New York aboard the SS Mauritania in September 1950. I was on my way to Europe on a traveling fellowship. As the ship passed a mere two miles off the jetty at Beach Forty-eighth Street, I could see my family standing on the bulkhead waving and unfurling a huge American flag. My mother finally left Sea Gate in 1986, ending my family's 67-year Sea Gate connection.

Joel Harnett

Joel Harnett lived at 4240 Surf Avenue. He graduated from Lincoln in 1942 and the University of Richmond in 1945. He served in the U.S. Army Reserve for nineteen years and retired with the rank of major. Joel was VP and marketing director of *Look Magazine* over a nineteen-year period, founder of Media Horizons, a public company in print and broadcast, and owner of radio stations WGBY in upstate New York and WRAN in New Jersey. He served as chairman of the City Club of New York and ran for mayor of New York in 1977. Joel served briefly in the Koch administration and later in Governor Mario Cuomo's administration. He created some news in the 1977 campaign when he sued the SEC (Securities Exchange Commission) for the results of their investigation of the city's finances. He won the case, which ultimately led to the defeat of Abraham Beame in the mayorial campaign.

Joel Harnett during his mayoralty campaign in 1972

Joel moved to Arizona and founded three successful magazines: *Phoenix House and Garden, Sports Arizona* and *Scottsdale Scene* (now *Scottsdale Life*). On September 22, 2001, the University of Richmond Museums inaugurated the Joel and Lila Harnett Print Study Center. This museum also includes the Marsh Art Gallery. Funding for the center has been provided by Joel and his wife, Lila. Prior to the museum's inauguration, Lila and Joel sponsored several one-person exhibitions of works by such notable American artists as George Tooker, Philip Pearlstein, Jerome Witkin, and Janet Fish.

Joel enjoys writing poetry and had several poems published about life in Arizona, New York City—"9/11 Plus 60," "The City Belongs to Me," and "Empire States"—and his reflections of childhood days in Sea Gate. Below is an excerpt from *The Lights of South Mountain*, a poem that brackets his life from Sea Gate to Phoenix.

> When I was very young a lighthouse beamed along the
>   ocean shore of my town, its sweeping ray warning of
>   rocks or shallows and, when the fog was high, casting
>   eerie, pale gold shadows.
> Near it bootleggers distilled their products in a beachfront
>   home and loaded them on ships under cover of the
>   scanning light.

One day Sea Gate awoke to the pungent, rummy odor of running booze, pumped into the streets by federal agents who found the still: a scandal! But not without a twinge of civic pride that such nefarious doings could happen here.

It was the bootleggers who led me to see it, to feel its baleful gaze and grasp its lonely mission over the featureless sea—to link it in memory with a time, a place.

It was a first-time memory, the base for all to come.

The lights of South Mountain. Lighthouse of Sea Gate seventy years apart. Fleeting margins of a passing life.

Kadish Millet

Kadish Millet has lived in Sea Gate most of his adult life. A prolific songwriter, he has composed over a thousand songs. Such artists as Bing Crosby, Katerina Valenti, Anthony Newley, Connie Francis, The Drifters, and Keely Smith have recorded two hundred of his songs. Like most Sea Gaters, he attended PS 188, Mark Twain Junior High, and Lincoln High. "Sea Gate is the place I was born, and grew up, receiving a wonderful education at these schools," said Millet. Kadish enrolled in Brooklyn College in 1941. When the Japanese attacked Pearl Harbor, he enlisted in the U.S. Army Signal Corps and was stationed at Ft. Monmouth, New Jersey. He served a tour of duty in Europe in 1944 and returned to Sea Gate in 1945 to resume his education at Brooklyn College. He developed an intense love for music and enjoyed composing and writing songs. On a whim, he entered a contest at Brooklyn College to compose a victory march and won the contest by a wide margin. He later enrolled in the MA degree program at NYU, majoring in French and elementary education and later teaching at PS 188 and Mark Twain. In addition to contemporary songs, he takes special pride in giving back to his community via writing fifteen "official" school songs for PS 188, PS 90, PS 329, Mark Twain, Lincoln, Kingsborough Community College and Brooklyn College. Many of his songs received national and international critical praise by music reviewers and critics. He appeared on WNYC, where they played some of his lilting tunes such as "Tribute to Baseball" and "Hockey." One of his most notable songs, "What's More American?" which was performed by—among others—bandleader Lawrence Welk, was played as a wake-up song for the astronauts aboard the space shuttle Columbia in 1990.

Kadish Millet

Bing Crosby liked Millet's "What's More American" so much that it became one of his best-remembered standards. The words to this song were sung, whistled, and hummed by countless patriotic Americans over the last twenty-five years, including the many celebratory ceremonies following 9-11.

What's More American?
Words and Music by Kadish Millet

What's more American than corn flakes?
The Fourth of July and Uncle Sam.

What's more American than baseball?
I am, I am, I am!

What's more American than toothpaste?
Rock and roll, peanut butter, toast and jam.
What's more American than OK?
I am, I am, I am!

The stars and stripes, George Washington,
The capitol dome and bubble gum.
There's General Grant, and Robert E. Lee,
But most of all you can count on little old . . .
Me, Me, Me.

What's more American than ice cream?
Chow mein, pizza pie, Virginia Ham.
What's more American than bingo?
I am, I am, I am!

Ours is a heritage second to none.
We are a nation united as one.
Our founding fathers gave us that start,
And their love for our country lives on in ev'ry
heart!

What's more American than football?
TV and mighty Superman?
What's more American than saying
I am, I am, I am!

Some other songs by Kadish Millet:

Always and Forever
Always Together
Blue Grass of Kentucky Meet
Captain of My Ship

Carbon Copy Kisses
Dinga Linga Ling
Gitchee Gumee
Hats Off
Hats Off to Broadway
Hope
June, July, August and September
Let's Rock and Roll
Lifetime of Happiness
My Church is My Palace
Only a Phone Call Away
Please Remember Me
Soldier of Fortune
Valentino
Voulez Vous Cha Cha
Young in Years

One of Kadish's favorites is "Hats Off to Brooklyn." Someday, he hopes, it will be as famous as "I Left My Heart in San Francisco," or "My Kind of Town (Chicago Is)." While the composer has an impressive career résumé, it still hasn't garnered the one goal that drives Millet daily—the naming of his song as the borough's official theme song. "Brooklyn ought to have a theme song," he told me. "A song will outlive all of us. It brings a sense of belonging to something, and the people of Brooklyn desperately need a sense of belonging."

Referring to "Hats Off to Brooklyn," Kadish reflected: "This borough is my roots. It's everything to me, and I want it to remain in the forefront forever. A song would make people aware that Brooklyn is alive and kicking.

"Brooklyn is truly unique. You can't write a slow ballad for a place like this," he adds. "Brooklyn is alive. Its people are sharp, quick, lively, and alert. 'You'll always know what's cookin' once you've been a part of Brooklyn'[32] is one of the lines that reflects this spirit."

Sea Gate Song

Marvin Minoff

Marvin Minoff lived in Sea Gate at 3844 Lyme Avenue. He graduated from Lincoln High in June 1949 and ventured west to California to seek opportunities in the entertainment world. He is married to actress Bonnie Franklin, who starred in the TV sitcom, *One Day at a Time*. Minoff spent fifteen years with such major agencies as William Morris and IFA (now ICM). He rose to become vice president of the motion picture department and handled such respected talents as Sidney Lumet, Cicely Tyson, David Rintels and Bruce Joel Rubin.

Marvin Minoff

Marvin Minoff's Home at 3844 Lyme Avenue in Sea Gate

After leaving the agency business in 1974, Marvin became president of David Frost's David Paradine Television, Inc., where he co-produced interviews with Henry Kissinger and the Shah of Iran. At David Paradine, he was also responsible for James Michener's *Dynasty,* starring Harrison Ford, Amy Irving, Sarah Miles, and Stacy Keach; *The Ordeal of Patty Hearst*; and *Diary of a Rebel: Margaret Sanger.*

Minoff's other television credits include the NBC summer show, *Headliners,* a three-hour network special; *A Gift of Song,* starring some of the biggest names in the music business, and about a dozen *The Guinness Book of World Records* specials for ABC. The latter, filmed all over the globe, set some sort of record itself when Minoff rented the Eiffel Tower and staged a race to the top.

In 1988 Marvin Minoff entered into a partnership with actor Mike Farrell. The first project of Farrell/Minoff Productions was the critically acclaimed feature film, *Dominick & Eugene,* released in March of that year by Orion Pictures Corporation

Marvin Minoff (seated at extreme right) with Sea Gate friends, circa 1949. Standing (left to right): Donald Flansbaum, Ronnie Berliner, Sonny Krown, Donny Brenner, and Barry Gell. Seated (left to right): Larry Levine, Walter Spodek, Sandy Einhorn, Phil Brenner, and Marvin Minoff. Photo courtesy of Rhoda Shapiro

Alfred Kaskel

Alfred Kaskel lived in Sea Gate from the early 1930s to the late 1940s. He first rented the upper floor of a modest three-family home on 3782 Surf Avenue, where he and his wife, Doris, raised their first child, Carole.

First Sea Gate Home, 3782 Surf Avenue

Alfred Kaskel's daughter, Carole (third from left) poses with Sea Gate friends near her home at 3782 Surf Avenue. From left to right: Sheila Brustein, Bernice Meyers, Carole Kaskel, Rella Meyers, Marilyn Ferber, and Donny Robins. Circa 1936.

With the birth of two other children, Anita and Howard,

the Kaskel family purchased their first home on Beach Forty-fifth Street.

Second Home: 4505 Beach Forty-fifth Street.

In the mid-'30s he realized the potential for real estate growth in New York City and its outer boroughs, providing affordable housing for an expanding population. Careful investments in modest properties in Brooklyn and Manhattan led to a real estate office in Manhattan, he became president of the 471 East Forty-Fifth Street Corporation. Al Kaskel then began developing tracts in the borough of Queens, especially in sites for six-story, elevated apartment buildings. In 1945 Alfred Kaskel bought the Belmont Plaza Hotel in Manhattan at Lexington Avenue and Forty-ninth Street, which marked the beginning of a rapid acceleration into the hotel real estate arena. Shortly thereafter, a new corporation was created to handle all of Kaskel's real estate activities—Carol Management—named after his oldest daughter, Carole. [note: the daughter is spelled with the "e" and the corporation is spelled without the "e."]

In 1947, Carol Management acquired the Half Moon Hotel, a Coney Island landmark on the Boardwalk, and the Bradford Hotel in Boston, Massachusetts, the former for $900,000.

The Kaskel family sold their home in Sea Gate and bought a luxury apartment on Fifth Avenue in Manhattan and a home in Stamford, Connecticut. Always alert for the next trend in real estate, Kaskel foresaw the burgeoning spa/resort and golf market as a new investment.

Alfred Kaskel, 1945

The Doral was the dream of Alfred and his wife, Doris, who combined parts of their first names to name the Doral Hotel and Country Club. In 1959 they bought 2,400 acres of swampland west of Miami; a luxurious facility resort opened there in 1962. The Kaskels added a tennis center in 1970, hiring friend and tennis great Arthur Ashe as the director of tennis.

After Alfred Kaskel died in 1968, son Howard and his associates at Carol Management, continued to stay ahead of the golf industry trends, adding a spa in 1987. In 1993, the KSL Recreation Corporation bought Doral. Doris Kaskel died in 1988.

Peter Spanakos

The journey of research for *Sea Gate Remembered: New York City's First Gated Community* began with scouring libraries, historic societies, museums, and search engines on the Internet. The one key name that appeared in much of the material relating to modern Sea Gate was Pete Spanakos. My first order of business was to meet him. In a phone call to the Sea Gate Association, community manager Lisa Hernandez gladly gave me Pete's number.

"Be delighted to meet with you," was Pete's response when I asked him for a brief interview. "Come on over to my house. I'll give you a tour, introduce you to some of Sea Gate's interesting residents, and will be glad to answer any of your questions."

At sixty-four, Pete has the physique of an ex-Mr. America body builder spokesman, hawking vegetable juice on late night TV infomercials. With a full head of thick gray hair, a broad smile, and a firm handshake, he welcomed me in his home. And what a home it was! As Sea Gate's leading resident, historian and unofficial "Mayor of Sea Gate," Spanakos talked glowingly about his adopted community, its history, and his pride and joy—his all-steel, waterfront home designed by William Van Alen. I remember having a curious fascination for that house over sixty years ago while visiting my childhood friend, Harvey Weiss, whose family lived down the same block on 5020 Ocean View Avenue.

"How did you find this house?" I asked. "I spotted an ad in the paper," Pete told me, "back in the fall of 1967."

ONE-OF-A-KIND HOME

SEA GATE, ALL-STEEL WATERFRONT, 3-BEDROOM HOME, CENTRAL AIR CONDITIONING, WITH BULKHEAD, PRIVATE BEACH, CABANA, RIPARIAN RIGHTS, EXCLUSIVE PRIVATE RESIDENTIAL COMMUNITY WITH PRIVATE: POLICE, SANITATION, CABANA-POOL COMPLEX, BEACHES, CHAPEL, SCHOOL, DAY CAMP, LIGHTHOUSE, PARKS AND BUS SERVICE. DRAMATIC DAY TIME VIEW OF SHIPS, BOATS, BIRDS, AND SUNSETS ON WATER. FANTASTIC EVENING VIEW OF

LIGHTED VERRAZANO BRIDGE, NYC SKYLINE, ALL-YEAR-ROUND VACATION SPOT. JUST 10 MILES AND 20 MINUTES TO MANHATTAN. THE GOLD COAST OF NYC. PRICE FIRM: $65,000.

The "Cube House" at 5100 Ocean View Avenue in Sea Gate

"When we looked at the house, we were so impressed with it and the community, that we instantly negotiated the price."

Peter Spanakos—the spelling derived from the fact that Pete has a twin brother and both of them chalked up KOs (knockouts) as national champion bantamweight boxers. Pete and his brother, Nikos, were raised in the Red Hook neighborhood of Brooklyn. Fighting was something of a necessity for survival on those rough streets. Pete and Nick also had to learn to defend themselves in a hurry because of their small size, or just because they were Greek.

"The Italian kids beat us up one day, and the next, the Irish beat us up, and then we said, 'Well, we're going to learn to fight.'"

They quickly learned the art of boxing, and honed their skill at local gyms. Never looking for fights, they stood up to bullies and the word spread rapidly throughout the neighborhood: Don't mess with the Spanakos boys.

Pete Spanakos

Eventually they decided to parlay their street-fighting skills into boxing careers and began boxing in gyms in and around Brooklyn. It didn't take long for Pete and Nikos to move up the boxing hierarchy:

- Won ten Golden Glove titles between them from 1955 to 1964 at 112, 118 and 126 pounds
- Won over forty boxing titles including the NCAA, AAU, Parks and PAL
- Pete won a bronze medal in the 1959 Pan-American Games
- Engaged in over two hundred career fights
- Inducted into the Athletic Hall of Fame of Albertson College of Idaho and AHEPA (Greek American Fraternal Organization)

Although Pete hung up his boxing gloves a long time ago, he still keeps ties with the boxing profession by serving on the Ring #8 Board of Trustees, an organization that helps boxers and helped establish the Bill Gallo College Scholarship for amateur boxers and Steve Acunto's A. A. I. B boxing group.

Pete often reflects how lucky he was to have pursued that unique Brooklyn realty ad back in 1967. As Pete and his wife, Niki, relax in their "sugar cube" home, they enjoy the blissful life with spectacular views of Gravesend Bay, Ambrose Channel, and lower Manhattan.

"At night, the stars sparkle and the entire Verrazano Bridge is lit up like a shimmering pearl necklace," Pete said.

Niki Spanakos added that because of the setting and fantastic view they would hate to move. "For me the best part is when the sky gets dark," she said, "and the white boats are rushing to get back against the dark sky." Spanakos, the founder and President of the Sea Gate Historical Society has given over 100 free Sea Gate tours.

Mary Elizabeth Dillon

> *As a little kid, I knew Mary Dillon. She was a good friend of my dad and I went to her home many times on Atlantic Avenue in Sea Gate. She loved to swim, but didn't want to go by herself. At the time, her husband, Henry Farber, was very ill, so my dad would go with her to the beach.*

This was Barbara Browne-Cramer's recollection of Mary Elizabeth Dillon. Mary was one of twelve children born in Greenwich Village, to Philip and Ann Eliza Dillon. There were seven boys and five girls. The children went to school as long as the family budget allowed and then went to work to help ease the financial burdens of a struggling family.

While attending PS 41, in Greenwich Village, Mary Dillon

modeled clothes for buyers in a local garment firm. It was her first job and her salary went right into the family budget.

The Dillon family moved from Greenwich Village to Coney Island in 1901. During the summers of 1902-3, Mary worked for $6 a week at Stauch's Bath House distributing bathing suits to customers. In 1903, her sister, Eva, quit her job as a clerk in the Brooklyn Borough Gas Company (which served all of the old town of Gravesend-Coney Island, Sheepshead Bay, Brighton Beach, and Sea Gate). Mary took Eva's place because Eva was to be married and the Dillon family needed the money. A senior at Erasmus Hall High School, she had to drop out and never finished. But Mary rose through the ranks and in 1926 became president and chairman of the board. No woman had ever held such a position in a major utility corporation. A soft-spoken, petite woman, Mary was only a shade over five feet in height and sat on a sofa pillow when photographers came to snap her behind her big desk—by all accounts ran the company with competency, firmness, and, graciousness. As the company's chief advocate and spokesperson for twenty-three years, she was equally comfortable talking with top CEOs, stockholders, employees, and a packed auditorium of gas company customers.

Miss Mary became a "Mrs." in 1935, marrying Sea Gater Henry Farber. In 1942, she scored another first by accepting Mayor LaGuardia's invitation to head the New York City Board of Education.

Over the years, when not behind her desk at the office, Mary Dillon found time to work on dozens of committees during Word War II and to decorate her beautiful home on Sea Gate's Atlantic Avenue. A photo of Mary Dillon appears with officers of the Sea Gate Lighthouse Canteen in chapter 6.

Teri Seidman

Terri Seidman

Terri lived at 3723 Nautilus Avenue. She attended PS 188, Mark Twain Junior High School, and Lincoln High School and graduated from Syracuse University. Teri is an award-winning interior designer, author, and speaker and has helped to define interior style for the Hamptons and New York City since the late 1980s. Her uniquely, exciting vision has been showcased in renowned projects such as the 1997 Drawing Room in the Long Island Mansions and Millionaires Show Houses and the Kaylie Center of the Hampton synagogue in Westhampton Beach.

In the 1990s, Seidman's two best-selling books, *Decorating Rich* and *Decorating for Comfort*, appeared on a Book of the Month Club list. She toured the country, appearing on television shows like *Oprah*, *Good Day, New York* and *CNN Style*, while many of her projects were featured in *HG*, *House Beautiful*, *Woman's Day*, *Ladies Home Journal*, *Redbook*, *Hong Kong Journal*, *Bride's*, *Newsday* and *The New York Times*, among others. For over twelve years she has been a columnist for *House* magazine and *Country Decorating*.

Teri relates some found memories of growing up in Sea Gate:

The one word that comes to mind when I think

about Sea Gate is joyfulness. *I was an only child, but I was never, ever lonely. It was a special place at a special time. It was about the emergence of television, the essence of our childhood, coming of age and the enduring quality of affection of friends and family.*

When my Uncle Mac returned from Europe with the Eighth Air Force, he showed us autographed photos of Betty Grable, Lana Turner and other USO celebrities who entertained the troops in Europe. My family decided to celebrate his homecoming with a block party on Nautilus Avenue. The street was cordoned off from Sea Gate Avenue to the gate on West Thirty-seventh Street. The day before, my family cooked and prepared marvelous dishes for the feast. The party went on all night and I remember going to bed early that August night. The next morning, I couldn't believe what I saw. The guests were sleeping on the lawn after drinking most of the night.

CHAPTER 9

GALLERY OF HOMES

The private gated community of Sea Gate begins where the streets and boardwalk of Coney Island end. Behind a twelve-foot-high, chain link fence, stretching along West Thirty-seventh Street from the ocean to the bay is a community of homes that vary from one and two-family brick structures to Mediterranean villas, beach houses, and rambling Victorians, many influenced by the architectural styling of Stanford White.

4715 Surf Avenue in Sea Gate. A Stanford White-designed home. Photo courtesy of Pete Spanakos

Before Sea Gate was so named, it was known as Coney Island Point and was looked upon as a sand hill. The first structure to be erected in 1840 was Mike Norton's old tavern on Gravesend Bay, and was patronized by the fishermen from the bay. The visionaries of the Norton's Point Land Company projected an idyllic place where home sites could be sold for a handsome profit. The company introduced improvements in roads, lighting and sewage and began an aggressive campaign to advertise and promote the sale of lots in Sea Gate. Turn-of-the-century newspaper articles carried stories with passages such as this in *The Brooklyn Eagle* on July 19, 1902.

> *That Sea Gate is a beautiful spot and at the same time a popular place of residence for those who can afford to pay a good price was demonstrated during the week just passed by the sale of about seventy lots in the most desirable section. Good prices were obtained and within the next year one may see many handsome houses erected on the property. If the Brooklyn Rapid Transport Company furnishes a good winter service it is thought many of those who now reside at Sea Gate will remain all winter.*
>
> *The Norton's Point Land Company has been introducing improvements at Sea Gate ever since the Atlantic Yacht Club house was erected and today the visitor will find many macadamized streets and avenues, as above stated, handsome houses by the hundreds.[33]*

Both 1902 and 1903 were banner years for property lot sales in Sea Gate. A "getting-in-on-the-ground-floor" philosophy motivated a surge of sales. Early real estate records showed that Charles Harris of Hoboken bought seven lots on the northwestern corner of Lyme Avenue and West Thirty-seventh Street; Charles Keinston purchased nine lots on Laurel Avenue; and Alice Lecouver purchased lots on the southeastern corner of Neptune Avenue and West Thirty-seventh Street and on Maple Avenue near West Thirty-seventh Street.

As homes were built in the early part of the century, Sea Gate's four and a half miles of winding tree-lined roads and nine miles of sidewalks gradually took on a character of their own. Streets were named in nautical and tree-related themes. Surf, Mermaid and Neptune were already named as extensions of Coney Island. Atlantic, Nautilus, Oceanic, Ocean View Avenues and the Beach Streets took on nautical themes, while Maple, Poplar, and Cypress were named after trees that were planted in Sea Gate at the time.

My family moved to Sea Gate in 1918. We lived on 3739 Oceanic Avenue. From Oceanic Avenue we had an unobstructed view of the ocean. Later, houses were built on Surf and Atlantic Avenues and we lost that wonderful view. Growing up I spent my summers on the beach. Most of the time, sitting on the rocks and making up stories about the seashell people imbedded in them. Lucille Markow and Beatrice Nussbaum were my friends.

Theda Backalenick-Frank, Lincoln High School 1933, Cornell 1937

My father was born in Austria and immigrated to America in 1920 where he settled in Sea Gate. He bought a house on the corner of Maple and Sea Gate Avenues. My family operated it as a hotel. It had a dining room, a wait staff and about thirty guest rooms. At the time, my father worked in the garment center as a clothing cutter and my mother took care of the hotel. The hotel operation lasted about eight years and my father decided to convert it into a rooming house. In order to save money, (we were very poor) the house was partially heated. Instead of paying for coal delivery we scoured the beach for driftwood to use as firewood.

*My brother and I collected the wood, brought it home,
cut it into smaller pieces and used it as fuel in the
winter. Unfortunately we slept on the third floor, which
remained unheated. The first and second floor was
used for rent-paying tenants and was heated. We
eventually sold it and moved to an apartment on
Atlantic Avenue near Beach Thirty-eighth Street.*

Noel Schwartz

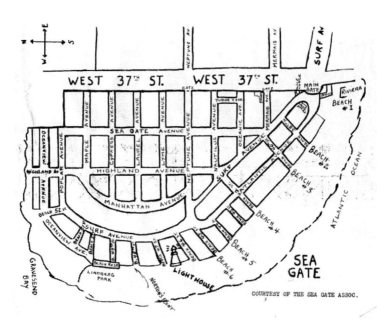

**Map of Sea Gate. Courtesy of the Sea Gate
Association**

But the era of glorious mansions with grand gardens and
porches did not last forever. Many single-occupancy mansions
owned by millionaires were gradually turned into multiple-family
dwellings during the Depression. Most of the grand houses that
pre-date the 1920s were built as summer residences and were not
economically suitable for today's lifestyle. Cool breezes from the
Atlantic Ocean—when available—helped to keep these summer

homes comfortable. Many of them however were not well suited for year-around occupancy.

I remember living in our home on Atlantic Avenue. My father would complain every month when he would receive the oil bill. We didn't need air-conditioning in the summer. I remember we all slept with a blanket even during July and August. During the winter, however, the poorly-insulated windows did not provide enough of a barrier for the winds that swept in from the ocean.

The former oceanfront mansion of Harry E. Verran at 4200 Atlantic Avenue was converted into the once-regal Floridian Hotel. It was gradually transformed into apartments and used as a meeting place for members of the Bund (a Jewish socialist organization) in the 1930s. Aliza Greenblatt, the mother-in-law of Woody Guthrie, the folk singer, remembered that Woody, who lived on Mermaid Avenue, would venture into the gate and visit with a group of poets and intellectuals who lived at the Floridian. "I remember my friend, Shirley Levine, lived at the Floridian after she returned from her honeymoon," recalls Pearl Hornreich. "She had a beautiful apartment and it was convenient for her family of 3 brothers and 5 sisters to visit because the Levine family lived across the street on Atlantic Avenue." In June 1942, David Tanenbaum the new owner, rebuilt the Floridian into a twenty-one-family house.

> *At one time Sea Gate was a tremendous resort community. We had hotels, and people flocked to them in the summers. The Floridian, which is now a rooming house, used to be a popular hotel back in the early thirties, and the Whittier Inn (now a senior residence) attracted the affluent crowd and their families. The Whittier was always filled to capacity. It had strict standards of dress. You could not walk into the dining room or the lobby without a jacket and tie. Rich Jewish families would go there to marry off their daughters.*
>
> **Harry Greenstein**

The Floridan Hotel on Atlantic Avenue and Beach
Forty-second Street still stands. Photo by Arnold
Rosen, January, 2003

Most of us who lived in the Gate were familiar with the Ocean
Breeze Hotel. It covered a whole block on Surf Avenue and had a
well-kept front lawn. In the last two decades of the century the
Ocean Breeze catered to orthodox Jews. The food and the cooking
were strictly *glatt kosher.* The hotel combined a beach and rural setting
with the convenience of being within city limits. In 1995 the former
stately hotel was transformed into the Abraham II residence for elderly
homeless people—including some recovering alcoholics and recently
arrived Russian-Jewish immigrants. The facility features manicured
grounds, new floors and ceilings, and in place of small hotel rooms
for summer visitors, one-room apartments equipped with kitchens
and baths. I recently interviewed Pearl Hornreich-Abramson, a 79-
year old resident who lives across the street (in the same house her
father bought when she was seven years old). She remembered the
rambling old building. "I loved that hotel as a kid. I remember the
Ocean Breeze would serve desserts to guests late on summer nights
and that my friends and I would sneak up to the outdoor tables and
steal cookies. It's a change for the better and I love it. It's beautiful
now."

Ex-Governor Al Smith lived next door to us, at
4810 Beach Forty-eighth Street, in a big black

shingled house. The house was demolished after the
war in favor of a group of small brick dwellings.
Leonard Everett Fisher

Now many new homeowners in Sea Gate have modernized their houses and changed them from multifamily to one or two-family homes. Some homebuyers find that it is cheaper to tear down the home completely rather than to begin a full-blown renovation. There are a few gems from the turn-of-the-century era but basically, Sea Gate is a very eclectic mixture of architectural styles that dates back 110 years with a mixture of contemporary, modern, and Victorian.

Mary Dillon's beautiful ocean front sprawling cottage home on Atlantic Avenue and Beach Fortieth Street was sold to the Dworman family. They kept the architectural integrity of the home intact. When the Dworman family moved out of Sea Gate they sold the home and were distressed to learn that the new owner planned to level the home and build a new one on the site.

I was devastated when he told me that he was
going to level the home. Our family loved that home.
It had such character. I suggested that we would remove
the home for him and transport it to another site. He
refused and indicated that he was in a hurry and
already contracted with a demolition company to start
work immediately. Ironically the demolition company
didn't start work for three months.
Darryl Dworman

Beach Thirty-eight Street between Surf and Atlantic Avenue consisted of three homes. Bart Meissner lived on the corner at Surf Avenue, Lester Martin occupied the middle home and on the corner at Atlantic and Beach Thirty-eight was a sprawling mansion, owned by a member of the Dupont family. The roof was all Spanish tile in terra cotta color and the walls were constructed in fine stone masonry. In addition to the main house, the property included a separate guest (or possibly a servant) house.

As kids we used to play punchball on the street and we always wondered about the people that lived inside. On rare occasions a chauffeured 1938 LaSalle limo would leave the garage and we caught glimpses of a Dupont matriarch in the back seat. When our Spaldeen ball bounced into her yard, we were reluctant to scale the fence surrounding the property. Signs posted along the fence warned intruders, "No trespassing. Beware of Dog." We lost many Spaldeens over the years in her yard.

A major restoration of a 6,000-square-foot Victorian on Atlantic Avenue was recently completed. The home, once home to a dozen families, was sold and the owner turned it into a one-family home. Some Sea Gate homes have a rich history. New owners have improved, expanded and redecorated.

In 1948 my family bought a three-story-Spanish-tile-roof, 16-room home at 4016 Atlantic Avenue from the Zieglebaum family.

My home at 4016 Atlantic Avenue, circa 1910.
Photo courtesy of the Brooklyn Historical Society

My mother redecorated the inside, converted smaller rooms into one large area, remodeled the kitchen and bathroom and installed a marble fireplace imported from Carrara, Italy. The outside façade was left intact to retain the original design. The house directly across the street, at 4015 Atlantic, once an elegant mansion, has been converted into multi-family rentals. Each Sea Gate home has its own, unique history. By searching the Sea Gate Association's archives, the history of 4015 reveals:

Original Owner: 1904, Charles Marchand, M.D., a physician, manufacturer, chemist, and pharmacist. He discovered a method of producing hydrogen peroxide. Dr. Marchand used his Atlantic Avenue mansion solely as a summer home.

Second Owner: 1924, Dr. Julius Benjamin, who also used the home as a summer resort. He named it the original *Ocean Breeze Hotel*.

Third Owner: 1947, first used the building as a summer resort. In June 1950, he completed conversion from the original sixteen rooms to the present twenty-five. A heating system was installed for year-round occupancy of rooms and apartments.

Fourth Owner: 1965, Manuel Litt, a horticulturist, updated and enclosed boiler room; installed aluminum storm windows and doors and did extensive front porch and cement block work on the foundation.

4015 Atlantic Avenue

The era of single occupancy (detached) homes was interspersed with the introduction of garden apartments. In June, 1950, the Harbor View Gardens opened at Sea Gate and Poplar Avenues. The three-story garden-type buildings contained thirty-six apartments of two, three, four and four and one-half rooms. The apartments with four and one-half rooms have two baths. This was Sea Gate's first attempt at development housing expansion. The buildings offered tenants TV outlets, concealed radiation and automatic laundry facilities.

With the influx of a diversified population, especially among Hasidic Jews, homes and apartments are at a premium in Sea Gate today.

Historic Landmarks: The Sea Gate Lighthouse

>*When I was young, I lived near the beach. My beach was at the beginning of the harbor of New York City. All the ships that had to go to New York City passed my beach.*
>
>*My street ended at the water and right there at the end of the street was a tall, white lighthouse. All night the lighthouse would shine a red light to warn the ships. "Stay away, stay away. The water is not deep here and there are rocks. If you come too close, you will get stuck in the sand of the beach and in the rocks. Stay away." This was what I imagined the lighthouse's beacon warned ships as they approached too close to Sea Gate's shoreline.*
>
>*The light turned all night. First it was shining out to the ocean, then on my street and its houses. Next it would shine on my house and my bedroom was filled with red light. It kept turning and the light went to the other side of the beach for a little while. Next the light was shining out to the ocean and the whole thing went on again and again. Every ten seconds the light made its turn. I liked it when the*

*light came into my room, because it meant that
everything was safe and good.*[34]

    *Our house was about fifty yards from the jetty.
Nothing stood between us and Staten Island but
the jetty, the Atlantic Ocean to our left, and
Gravesend Bay to our right. We lived on Norton's
Point with a clear and unobstructed front porch
view of all that passed in and out of New York by
water. A block away was the Norton's Point
Lighthouse.*[35]

Leonard Everett Fisher

**Leonard Everett Fisher's home on 4810 Beach
Forty-eighth Street**

Photo of the Lighthouse by Richard Rubinstein

The Norton's Point Lighthouse was first lit on August 1, 1890, for the U.S. Coast Guard, and is still in use, as the last manned lighthouse on the East Coast. It is situated between Beach Forty-seventh and Forty-eighth Streets in Sea Gate and can be seen from miles away by ship captains as they steer into New York Harbor and motorists driving on Brooklyn's Belt Parkway along the narrows. It is an imposing, eighty-foot-high white skeletal tower, consisting of a central steel column with eighty-seven steps, black gallery and lantern. The lighthouse has an original optic lens that flashes red every ten seconds. The caretaker is Frank Schubert, eighty-six years old, the last civilian lighthouse keeper in the country.

Pete Spanakos and I visited Frank one day. We talked briefly to him and he was affable and talked about some of the tribulations of being a lighthouse keeper.

> *In 1937 I worked as a crewman on the buoy boat fleet. The buoy boats sailed along the coast from Cape May, New Jersey to Newport, Rhode Island providing lighthouse keepers with supplies. In 1939 the US Coast Guard took over the buoy boat run and they fired all civilians. I started tending lighthouses that same year and have been here in Sea Gate since 1960.*
>
> *I'm the last civilian manning a lighthouse in the country; so what? Visitors and reporters coming around at all hours constantly bother me. They shoot film for hours and then call me back and say they want to shoot some more. They want me to climb up so they can film me. That's 87 steps. I've been up there enough times. I don't need to make any extra trips. I'm 86 and sometimes I say I should just chuck it. I've got a son in New Mexico. He wants me to come out there to live with him. But there's no water there. I've spent my whole life around water.*
>
> **Frank Schubert**

We talked on his back porch as his cocker spaniel cavorted in the big yard that extends to the bulkhead on the shoreline of Gravesend Bay. As we talked, I gazed at the horizon and noticed two little strips of islands rising midway from the waters between the Staten Island shores and Sea Gate. When I asked Frank about the islands he identified them as Hoffman and Swinburne Islands. Actually these small islands are man made and barely thirteen acres long. They are extinct now but during the active period of Ellis Island, they were used as quarantine and detention centers for immigrants. Swinburne Island served mostly as a quarantine hospital for those clearly showing airborne infectious diseases such as typhus, yellow fever, or smallpox. Hoffman Island served mostly as a quarantine for those exposed to the people put into medical quarantine on Swinburne.

"What's on the islands now?" I asked. "It's completely abandoned," Frank replied. "It's overgrown with weeds, a few abandoned buildings and a booming rat population, some the size of my pet cocker spaniel," he half-joked.

Frank Schubert, outside his cottage, talking to Pete Spanakos. Scaffold surrounds lighthouse for painting. Photo 11/19/2002 by Arnold Rosen

I first lived on Beach Forty-sixth Street across from the lighthouse and the World War II army installation of barracks, tents, marching soldiers and cannons protecting New York Harbor. I remember the "Greenhouse," the largest and most impressive shingled house in Sea Gate, which stood at the intersection of Neptune, Surf, and Atlantic Avenues. Dr. Joseph Wunsch wanted to save this house and donate it to the Brooklyn Museum for artists' studios. The museum refused the donation and the house was demolished.

Adrian Bouvier, the lighthouse keeper's son was my first childhood friend in Sea Gate. We would climb the steps together each evening to the top of the lighthouse to rewind the cable which had a weight attached to power the electric generator, which provided energy for the giant rotating Fresnel lens and light

Bob Tannen.

Dr. Wunch was an industrialist who built a house overlooking Gravesend Bay. He was an engineer and participated in the design of the Brooklyn Battery Tunnel. In addition, most of the beautiful antique furniture in the state department building in Washington, D.C., was donated by his family. He developed an interest in sculpture upon retirement from the Silent Hoist Crane Manufacturing firm in Brooklyn, which he founded. Dr. Joseph Wunsch was a close personal friend of Regina Orans, who introduced him to Bob Tannen. Bob, at the time, was constructing large abstract wood piles on Sea Gate beaches made of drift timbers and pieces of ships and docks, which had floated down the Hudson and East Rivers to Sea Gate. They both discussed the idea of creating a sculpture to be placed at the entrance of Sea Gate.

Bob Tannen made a piece of two abstractlike dancers out of eight hundred pounds of clay on a steel armature in his father's garage. This model was then cast in concrete and now stands proudly in the garden at the entrance of the Sea Gate Community

Center This project was a collaboration of a 70-plus-year-old and a 19-year-old sculptor who remained friends until the death of Dr. Wunsch. Harriet Harnett relates an amusing story about Dr. Wunsch:

> *Al Goldstein attended an opening of a special exhibit at the Metropolitan Museum of Art. He overheard someone greet this man, "Good evening, Mr. Wunsch!" Al walked over and asked, "Excuse me, are you the Mr. Wunsch from Sea Gate?" "Yes, I am!" the man replied. "Oh, I went to Abraham Lincoln High School with your son, Martin," he said. The man looked at Al Goldstein and said, "I am Martin!"*

A typical Sea Gate street. Laurel Avenue circa 1949. This photo was taken in front of 3826 Laurel Avenue looking northeast. The big house across the street (second from the left) with the frieze over the door belongs to Benjamin Salzhauer. He lived at 3815 Laurel Avenue. Photo courtesy of Kalman Bergen.

CHAPTER 10

SEA GATE TODAY

A Last Spin

The structure at the main gate at Surf Avenue looked somewhat familiar as an old timer like myself approached it after fifty years. Never mind that brick has replaced the shingled, wooden facing and the cylindrical two-story domed-topped edifice that housed the Sea Gate Police is now a brick structure.

Main Gate

The office of the Sea Gate Association is attached to the opposite side of the main gate. I identified myself as a visitor and was directed to park in the field on Surf Avenue, which we used to play softball sixty years ago. Community Manager Lisa Cosme-Hernandez directed me to use a large conference room and brought us up to date on *Sea Gate Today.*

Lisa Cosme-Hernandez

The association basically functions as it did at the turn of the century, though now it is a non-profit corporation with a $2 million annual budget. This goes toward its own state-licensed police force plus office staff and street maintenance. The city provides sanitation and additional police, fire and health services. The Sea Gate Maintenance/Sanitation Department employs four men, headed by supervisor Albert Berrios. This department is responsible for street maintenance, street cleaning, sewer maintenance, tree trimming, snow removal, fence maintenance, keeping up community facilities as well as beach cleaning and maintenance. The association has recently purchased a "sewer jetter"—a device that cleans and flushes sewers when they become clogged. Homeowners automatically belong to the association and pay annual dues based on assessed value of their homes, in addition to the city's real estate taxes. Most of the homes are one and two-family detached structures. A few Stanford White-influenced models still stand on the original sites along Surf and Atlantic Avenues. Others sit in seaside, flower-filled gardens, many under gigantic ancient trees, on manicured lawns, and some boast private beaches.

Pete Spanakos' home (described in chapter 8) is an all-steel, prefabricated waterfront home (with pier) designed by William Van Alen, who was the chief architect of the Chrysler Building, the iconic grandfather of art deco skyscrapers. It was reassembled from its original site on Park Avenue and Thirty-ninth Street in 1936 and later put up in Sea Gate facing the bay, the Verrazano Bridge and the New York skyline.

Time and weather have not been kind to a number of turn-of-the century houses. Deterioration has set in and some owners have turned them into multi-family dwellings. Donald Nier, a real estate agent in Sea Gate, sees a newer trend in local market. "Some new owners are modernizing houses and changing them from multi-family back into one or two families," he said.

Waterfront homes along the water range from $350,000 for a "handyman" special to several million dollars for seaside villas. Waterfront property is scarce and valuable. No empty waterfront lots presently exist along Atlantic and Ocean View Avenues.

A Changing Population

A diverse population, of mostly upper-middle class professionals, calls Sea Gate, home. About ten years ago, a small community of Hasidic Jews settled here. Recently, young families of Russian (mostly from the Odessa area of the old Soviet Union), Italian and Greek background have bought homes, and other ethnic groups such as African-Americans, Asians, and Hispanics rent or own property in Sea Gate.

Shopping, Recreation, and Cultural Activities

Inside the gate, there is no longer a food market. Residents can walk a block to Key Food from the Neptune Avenue gate or five blocks from either gate to Pioneer on Mermaid Avenue. If they choose to drive, Pathmark, on Cropsey Avenue and Edwards, on Avenue Y and East Seventeenth Street, are both open twenty-four hours a day. Although the fruit markets and delis have left Mermaid Avenue there are plenty of similar shops under the El on Brighton Beach Avenue and at Eighty-sixth Street in Bensonhurst.

> *Elderly people in Sea Gate seem to be very functional. Many of them still drive cars, even those in their late 80s. They also have relatives and friends who help with shopping and errands. For those who do not own cars, there are car services available and some seniors opt to live near Surf and Neptune Avenue gates, where they can walk the few blocks to food stores or pharmacies.*
>
> **Donald Nier**

For dining out, old standbys Gargiulo's and Carolina's still remain for homemade pasta and delicious Italian specialties. Retro, a newly renovated Greek diner on Cropsey Avenue, Russian restaurants in Brighton Beach, and Lundy's in Sheepshead Bay are other favorites.

Sea Gaters can enjoy a secure and relaxed lifestyle featuring many water sports. The ambiance and magnificent vistas provide an idyllic backdrop for jogging, bicycling, roller skating, or simply strolling along the beaches with gorgeous sunsets and breathtaking views of the Verrazano Bridge, the Manhattan skyline, Lower Manhattan, and Gravesend Bay.

Outside the Gate, Sea Gaters can jog and walk along the 2.5-mile Boardwalk and elsewhere in Coney Island, go ice-skating at Abe Stark Recreation Center on weekends from October to March or catch a dolphin show at the New York Aquarium on Surf Avenue. The Brooklyn Cyclones, a New York Mets minor league team, recently opened a first-class 6,500-seat stadium on the old Steeplechase Park site.

Coney Island's Rennaisance

Since the new KeySpan Stadium (home of the Brooklyn Cyclones baseball team) opened a few years ago, Coney Island's surrounding amusement area has been going through a rebirth. The ballpark has been an impetus for the city and concessionaires to expand, improve, and invest in the area. A new subway terminal at Stillwell and Surf Avenue is undergoing a $200 million facelift. When it is finished in 2005, city planners predict it will be a glorious portal to a great amusement center. Owners of the famed 83-year-old Wonder Wheel have refurbished their ride and its surrounding amusement park with a new 12,000-square-foot deck, added metal railings and wooden platforms for the twenty-five rides, repainted the big wheel structure and installed 400-watt spotlights to ignite the Coney Island night. The boardwalk has been repaired and the Cyclone roller coaster is now a landmark.

The famed Parachute Jump, Brooklyn's Eiffel Tower, is undergoing a major restoration. This 250-foot city landmark, which was moved to the boardwalk after the 1939 World's Fair and closed in the '60s when Steeplechase Park closed, was recently reassembled after extensive painting and repairing. Borough President Marty Markowitz is spearheading a plan to make it operational again. Adding a Parachute Jump ride to the Aquarium, Astroland, the Wonder Wheel, Cyclones stadium and a new subway station will go a long way toward Coney Island's rebirth as the Borough's premier amusement center.

The Sea Gate Beach Club

The same beckoning beach and dwelling ocean that once drew families and teenagers toward the shore some sixty and more years ago attracts today's Sea Gate residents. The epicenter is the new and expanded Sea Gate Beach Club. In 1996 the Sea Gate Association leased the cabana/pool complex to Fortune Financial and Investment Corporation. The complex features cabanas, a restaurant (now Big Boo's), an outdoor Tiki Bar, Olympic-size pool, Roman-style steam bath, beach and poolside cabanas, and organized activities for children.

Sea Gate Beach Club

Bruce Akrongold, president of Fortune Financial, describes the events that led him to invest in restoring the Riviera and Beach Club complex:

> *We originally came to Sea Gate to build a senior citizen housing facility on the site. Our broker indicated to us that was the intention of the Sea Gate Association. When we met with them there appeared to be a change of heart and now the board wanted a modern beach club. At first we told them that we didn't know much about running a beach club facility but the more we thought about it the more we came to realize that this was a wonderful piece of property on a great location and we decided to enter into an agreement with the association to develop it.*
>
> *Prior to our negotiations Sea Gate persuaded the federal government to undertake a beach restoration project after the storms of 1992 and 1993. A jetty was built to keep the sand intact and to stem the erosion of the beaches.*
>
> *We started work in March 1995. The place was an eyesore. The concrete deck was destroyed and the*

*Riviera restaurant facility was in disrepair. We
installed all new concrete on the deck, landscaped the
grounds, and began a major overhaul of the restaurant.
By Memorial Day, the sun was shining, the work was
complete, and we were ready to open our doors.*

The Sea Gate Association owns the property and Fortune
Financial leases and operates the beach club. As tenants, they
provide summer employment for college and high school students
who serve as waiters, waitresses, children's counselors and
lifeguards. The lifeguards watch over the pool and beaches and
operate under strict safety standards set up by the City of New
York and the American Red Cross.

*Our membership consists of Sea Gate residents
and others outside the Gate. Once inside the club,
people forget they are in Brooklyn. "This is
Brooklyn's best kept secret," some members say. It's a
nice compliment, but we really don't want to keep
the club a secret. We get people from all over Brooklyn
who visit friends in the Gate and say, "I never knew
this was here." Everyone knows there are still beach
clubs in Long Island and Rockaway and that the
Brighton Beach Baths and Palm Shores have closed,
but few know there is our beautiful club right here
in Brooklyn.*

Sal Argano, General Manager

*When we improved and rehabilitated the club it
gave the community a needed "shot in the arm." We
landscaped the grounds and gave the cabanas and
restaurant a fresh coat of paint, the place took on an
aura of a "shining star." It's one of the first things that
people see when they enter the gate and it really makes
a positive "first impression" of Sea Gate.*

Bruce Akrongold

Improvements on the Way

Beaches: The Army Corps of Engineers has devised a plan to help restore the reach of Sea Gate's beaches. The plan has three goals: (1) protect the West Thirty-seventh Street groin; (2) avoid erosion of sand from the beaches (judged by the 1998 shoreline), and (3) reduce the accumulation of sand in Gravesend Bay. The plan calls for building three T-shaped groins, one L-shaped groin and one "Spur" groin in the ocean. Replenishment of Sea Gate's beaches is also included in the plan. When complete, Sea Gate's beaches will upgrade the beauty, safe swimming and protection for the shoreline and community.

Parks: Parental concerns about the Dave Sevush Children's Park next to the old tennis court field between Surf and Mermaid Avenues, prompted the board of directors to form a "parks" committee, which determined that the equipment was outdated, no longer up to code, in disrepair and no longer able to meet the needs and desires of the children of Sea Gate. As a result, the playground has been cleared and plans were in the works for a new, safe and enjoyable place for the children. This plan included new and separate areas for younger children and older children to play and acquisition of new equipment.

A long forgotten and ignored area of Sea Gate, **Lindy Park**, is also in need of serious attention. At present it exists as an empty, undeveloped three-acre lot near where the Atlantic Yacht Club once reigned supreme. The board is in the process of formulating a plan for the future development of this neglected waterfront highlight so that the community as a whole can benefit from and enjoy it.

Sea Gate's fishing enthusiasts still use Lindy Park as a haven. They cast their lines along the rock jetties. With the new environmental protection laws, the Atlantic has been cleaner and recent catches include striped bass and fluke as well as crab and clams.

Ex-Sea Gaters and newcomers alike say that once they experience Sea Gate's secluded charm, they couldn't imagine living anywhere else in the city.

At dawn the Sea Gate vista reminds me of the opening line of The Iliad *by Homer when he describes "As the rose fingered dawn."*

The orange-red sunsets over Staten Island illuminates the sky with such beautiful colors that would add dimension to any box of crayons. At the mouth of New York Harbor, we can see the twin forts—Fort Hamilton in Brooklyn, and Fort Wadsworth on Staten Island.

I love it here! This lifestyle can't be beat! The streets are safe, quiet, and clean-where else can you get that? Sea Gate, to use Lou Powsner's metaphor, is no longer 'surrounded by an ocean of neglect and a bay of despair.'

Peter Spanakos

My husband, Bill, and I love Manhattan but we love returning home, too. The quiet, the fresh air, the clean smell of the ocean, and the tranquility is what we enjoy most. Sometimes we take a bike ride at night and you feel the ocean breezes and you say, "Wow, this is pretty good for New York City."

Billie Tannen

I remember those wondrous days growing up in Sea Gate. Some of the memories are poignant and wistful and they are like a time machine taking us back to such a degree that I can really smell the salt air and feel the warm sun on my skin as I drowse on a beach blanket, or sense the autumn leaves falling all around us, the taste of honeysuckle, the sound of bellbouys or the sight of the lighthouse light, the bus driver, cop or shopkeeper plus our friends, teachers, and family

Martha Warshaw.

Over the years, the neighborhood's fortunes have fluctuated, but today, proud Sea Gate folks say the neighborhood is thriving. All seem to agree that their secluded, wave-licked, gated community still remains one of Brooklyn's hidden treasures.

END NOTES

Chapter 1

1   The water at Sea Gate in 1900 came from artesian wells at Gravesend and passed through a natural filter of fine gravel.
2   The word "apartment" was used in that era. In present day usage it would be known as a cabana.
3   Courtesy of the Sea Gate Association
4   *The New York Times*, August 14, 1898

Chapter 2

5   Schulman, Sam, **Gate To The Sea.** *The Magpie*. Selections from the DeWitt Clinton High School's Literary Magazine, 1929-1942

Chapter 3

6   Fisher, Leonard Everett, *The Jetty Chronicles*, published by Marshall Cavendish, 1997, page 12.
7   Sills, Beverly, *Beverly, An Autobiography*, published by Bantam Books, 1985, pages 30-31.
8   Conroy, Pat, *My Losing Season*, published by Nan A. Talese, an imprint of Doubleday, 2002

Chapter 4

9   Richard Rubinstein wrote this narrative on his web site. He lived on Beach Forty-seventh Street in Sea Gate. Richard passed away on September 2, 2001. Permission to use this narrative was granted by his sister, Diana Wiener-Rubinstein.

10 Fisher, Leonard Everett, *The Jetty Chronicles*, published by Marshall Cavendish, 1997

Chapter 5

11 Klein, Joe, *Woody Guthrie: A Life*, published by Alfred A. Knopf, New York, 1980, page 333

12 Before public-housing projects loomed over Surf Avenue, Mermaid Avenue bustled with more than 400 prosperous retail businesses. By the 1980s, only 39 stores remained. Today, it may be Coney Island's bleakest area.

13 Klein, Joe, *Woody Guthrie: A Life*, published by Alfred A. Knopf, New York, 1980, page 307

14 Fisher, Leonard Everett, *The Jetty Chronicles*, published by Marshall Cavendish, 1997, pages 72-73

Chapter 6

14a "The Words and Music of World War II," An aural history on 2 CDs. Columbia Legacy, 1991 SONY Music Entertainment, Inc., manufactured by Columbia Records.

15 In contrast to what would happen today, neither the CBS nor NBC radio network interrupted regular programming-a musical variety show on CBS, Sammy Kaye on NBC Red and "Great Plays" on NBC Blue-to read the bulletin. NBC's Robert Eisenbach read a short bulletin at 2:30 before the network resumed regular programming. NBC did an hour-long news special in the evening.

16 War bonds became the standard gift for bar mitzvahs during the war years.

17 Wartime tobacco allocations referred to "legal" limits. But there was also another way: through the **Black Market**, a strictly underground industry

that sprung up to illegally supply consumers' hunger-at a price-for restricted products.

18 Sills, Beverly, *Beverly An autobiography*, published by Bantam Books, 1987, pp. 26-27.

19 "City Blacked Out On Atlantic Coast," *The New York Times*, March 20, 1942.

20 Pilat, Oliver and Ranson, Jo, *Sodom by the Sea*, published by Garden City Publishing Co., Inc., Garden City, NY., 1941 p.147

21 Fisher, Leonard Everett, *The Jetty Chronicles*, published by Marshall Cavendish, 1997, page 13

22 For some reason, the Navy wanted Sea Gate as the designated address.

23 "Hotel to be Hospital," *The New York Times*, August 26, 1944.

24 Words by Nat Burton, Music by Walter Kent, 1941

25 Originally Sea Gate had tennis courts in the early part of the twentieth century. It was a large triangular area bounded by West Thirty-seventh Street on the East, Mermaid Avenue on the North, and Surf Avenue on the Southwest. Enthusiasm for tennis waned in the late twenties and early thirties and gradually the field became the playground for softball and, to a lesser extent, football.

Chapter 7

26 Ironically, the Sea Gate Association announced a month before the storm that the Surf Avenue bus line was to be extended through Sea Gate along the existing route and from Sea Gate through Coney Island.

27 See Chapter 4, "I Remember," for narrative accounts of these events.

28 Stanley Ferber used to live at 3774 Surf Avenue

Chapter 8

29 Jackson, Kenneth and Manbeck, John,. *The Neighborhoods of Brooklyn*. Yale University Press, 1998, page 192

30 Singer, Isaac Bashevis, *Love and Exile, A Memoir*, published by Doubleday

& Company, 1984

31   Singer, Isaac Bashevis, *Love and Exile, A Memoir*, published by Doubleday & Company, 1984

32   Courtesy of Kadish Millet. "Hats Off To Brooklyn," words and music By Kadish Millet, published by Blue Umbrella Publishing Company (ASCAP). Telephone interview with Kadish on November 18, 2002

Chapter 9

33   "First Four-Story flat Built under the Present Law," *Brooklyn Eagle*, July 19, 1902

34   Richard Rubinstein wrote this narrative on his web site. He lived on Beach Forty-seventh Street, in Sea Gate. Richard passed away in 2001

35   Fisher, Leonard Everett, *The Jetty Chronicles*, published by Marshall Cavendish, 1997, page 12.

Chapter 10

APPENDIX

Where We Once Lived

Abbey, Naomi—4222 Surf Avenue
Achenbaum, Annette—3819 Cypress Avenue
Achenbaum, William—3832 Maple Avenue
Altman, Ethelind—3844 Lyme Avenue
Altman, Ronald—4111 Manhattan Avenue
Anolick, Lenore—3904 Laurel Avenue
Anolik, Judy—4010 Sea Gate Avenue
Arenson, Ted—3746 Maple Avenue
Ashenazy, Irving—4714 Surf Avenue
Ausubel, Jeanne—4211 Highland Avenue
Bachman, Victor—4202 Highland Avenue
Backalenick, Billie—3739 Oceanic Avenue
Backalenick, Theda—3739 Oceanic Avenue
Bader, Helen—3732 Lyme Avenue
Baker, Dan—3920 Lyme Avenue
Barbolla, Michael—3731 Poplar Avenue
Barkan, Harriet—4404 Atlantic Avenue
Barkan, Joyce—4404 Atlantic Avenue
Becker, Mickey—3829 Oceanic Avenue
Bell, Richard—3904 Neptune Avenue

Berg, Corrine—4411 Sea Gate Avenue
Bergen, Arlene—3718 Neptune Avenue
Bergen, Kalman—3718 Neptune Avenue
Berger, Irwin—3733 Laurel Avenue
Berkoer, Ruth—3847 Nautilus Avenue
Berlin, Joan—3792 Surf Avenue
Berliner, Ron—4005 Sea Gate Avenue
Brenner, Don—3729 Lyme Avenue
Brenner, Gloria—3729 Lyme Avenue
Brenner, Phil—3729 Lyme Avenue
Brill, Barbara—4209 Manhattan Avenue
Brody, Arthur 3743 Neptune Avenue
Broude, Joan—4226 Surf Avenue
Browne, Barbara—4703 Beach 47th Street
Browne, Eugene—4703 Beach 47th Street
Buxbaum, David—4209 Manhattan Avenue
Cantor, Mel—4208 Sea Gate Avenue
Christian, Paul—3832 Laurel Avenue
Cohen, Judy—3855 Nautilus Avenue
Cohen, Marilyn—3844 Poplar Avenue
Cullen, Ruby—3726 Laurel Avenue
Deitch, Toby—4505 Surf Avenue
Deutsch, Dorothy—4817 Beach 48th Street
Deutsch, Jerry—4817 Beach 48th Street
Deutsch, Sidney—4817 Beach 48th Street
DeWitt, Fay—3814 Sea Gate Avenue
Dolgenos, Dave—3817 Laurel Avenue
Drachman, Winifred—3848 Maple Avenue
Dreizin, Ruth—3845 Neptune Avenue
Dworman, Darryl—4906 Surf Avenue
Edwards, Rhoda—3841 Neptune Avenue
Ehrman, Beryl—3705 Neptune Avenue
Einhorn, Sanford—4716 Beach 47th Street
Engel, Muriam—3855 Nautilus Avenue
Ente, Paulette—3738 Lyme Avenue
Enver, Umit—4246 Surf Avenue

Esrig, Melvin—3833 Neptune Avenue
Esterces, Howard—3745 Cypress Avenue
Fahn, Barry—3712 Cypress Avenue
Feinberg, Cynthia—3846 Neptune Avenue
Feinberg, Eddie—3827 Oceanic Avenue
Ferber, Marilyn—3774 Surf Avenue
Ferber, Stanley—3774 Surf Avenue
Fink, Geraldine—3908 Laurel Avenue
Finkelstein, Shep—4012 Surf Avenue
Firester, Lee—3742 Cypress Avenue
Firester, Rosalie—3742 Cypress Avenue
Fisher, Leonard Everett—4810 Beach 48th Street
Fishman, Selma—4518 Beach 45th Street
Flam, Eli—4022 Surf Avenue
Flam, Mildred—4022 Surf Avenue
Flansbaum, Donald—3752 Laurel Avenue
Fogel, Anne—3736 Oceanic Avenue
Foshko, Jack—3844 Maple Avenue
Frank, Albert—3786 Surf Avenue
Frank, Bernard—3786 Surf Avenue
Frank, Herbie—4246 Surf Avenue
Frankel, Daniel—36 Tudor Terrace
Frankel, Elaine—3748 Poplar Avenue
Frankel, Francine—3748 Poplar Avenue
Frankel, Laurie—36 Tudor Terrace
Freedman, Irma—3940 Lyme Avenue
Freilich, Toby—3792 Surf Avenue
Friedland, Gloria—3723 Poplar Avenue
Friedman, Dan—4106 Highland Avenue
Friedman, Lenny—3792 Surf Avenue
Friedman, Philip—3792 Surf Avenue
Gabay, Edward—4401 Beach 44th Street
Gell, Barry—3836 Lyme Avenue
Gell, Richard—3836 Lyme Avenue
Gersh, Robert—4000 Highland Avenue
Gershunoff, Marion—4043 Atlantic Avenue

Glick, Joseph—3718 Laurel Avenue
Goldberg, Eugene—3920 Cypress Avenue
Goldberg, Frances—4817 Beach 48th Street
Goldberg, Maurice—3848 Nautilus Avenue
Goldberg, Michael—4817 Beach 48th Street
Goldreich, Carole—4621 Beach 46th Street
Goldreich, Louis—4621 Reach 46th Street
Goldrich, Stuart—3826 Nautilus Avenue
Goldstein, Al—3841 Cypress Avenue
Goldstein, Harris—3718 Surf Avenue
Goldstein, Jeff—4505 Beach 45th Street
Goldstein, Martha—3718 Maple Avenue
Goldstein, Sandra—3842 Maple Avenue
Goldstein, Sol—4246 Surf Avenue
Greenberg, Irwin—3722 Poplar Avenue
Greenstein, Evalyn—4409 Atlantic Avenue
Greenstein, Stanley—4409 Atlantic Avenue
Grinberg, Eugene—4915 Surf Avenue
Gross, Morty—4601 Beach 46th Street
Guerney, Bernard—4905 Surf Avenue
Haberman, Sylvia—4016 Highland Avenue
Halpert, Marlene—4626 Beach 46th Street
Harnett, Barbara—3907 Lyme Avenue
Harnett, Harriet—3907 Lyme Avenue
Harnett, Joel—4240 Surf Avenue
Harnick, Gloria—3841 Maple Avenue
Hassman, Larry—3728 Maple Avenue
Herman, Barbara—3792 Surf Avenue
Herzog Roslyn—5100 Surf Avenue
Hirsch, Stanley—3724 Oceanic Avenue
Hoch, Doris—4111 Sea Gate Avenue
Hodash, Stanley—4814 Atlantic Avenue
Horowitz, Deborah—4208 Manhattan Avenue
Israel, Deena—3834 Neptune Avenue
Israel, George—3834 Neptune Avenue
Jacobowitz, Muriel—3763 Nautilus Avenue

Jacobson, Irwin—3841 Neptune Avenue
Jacoby, Ruth—3763 Nautilus Avenue
Kahn, Herbert—3814 Lyme Avenue
Kaskel, Anita—4505 Beach 45th Street
Kaskel, Carole—4505 Beach 45th Street
Kastenbaum, Bernie—3816 Surf Avenue
Katcher, Paul—4202 Surf Avenue
Katz, Bernard—4311 Atlantic Avenue
Katz, Iris—4314 Sea Gate Avenue
Katz, Samuel—3842 Neptune Avenue
Kaufman, Ethel—4205 Sea Gate Avenue
Klein, Carol—4810 Surf Avenue
Korn, Monroe—3913 Sea Gate Avenue
Kramer, Ellen—3838 Popular Avenue
Kransdorf, Jacqueline—4034 Surf Avenue
Krawitz, Rhoda—4311 Sea Gate Avenue
Kronenberg, David—3708 Oceanic Avenue
Krown, Eleanor—4201 Sea Gate Avenue
Krown, Mel—4201 Sea Gate Avenue
Kublick, Gloria—4000 Highland Avenue
Lanster, Sol—4407 Beach 44th Street
Leibowitz, Harold—4405 Highland Avenue
Leibowitz, Martin—3714 Lyme Avenue
Lerner, Frank—4202 Surf Avenue
Levine, Carl—4051 Atlantic Avenue
Levine, Corrine—3814 Surf Avenue
Levine, Judy—4304 Highland Avenue
Levine, Lawrence—4315 Sea Gate Avenue
Levine. Sandy—4011 Sea Gate Avenue
Levinson, Irving—3782 Surf Avenue
Levitt, Martin—3766 Surf Avenue
Lipson, Diane—3829 Nautilus Avenue
Lipson, Naomi—3829 Nautilus Avenue
Mancene, Dorothy—3734 Poplar Avenue
Mancene, Lorraine—3734 Poplar Avenue
Mann, Eddie—3917 Sea Gate Avenue

Manusov, Eugene—4814 Surf Avenue
Markowitz, Roslyn—3727 Nautilus Avenue
Marquit, Malcolm—3825 Laurel Avenue
Martin, Eugene—3782 Surf Avenue
Martin, Jane—3823 Beach 38th Street
Martin, Robert—3823 Beach 38th Street
Meissner, Barton—3829 Beach 38th Street
Mennen, Carole—3819 Cypress Avenue
Metzger, Dorothy—4101 Sea Gate Avenue
Metzger, Reed—4104 Sea Gate Avenue
Meyerhoff, Lee—3840 Laurel Avenue
Meyers, Bernice—3796 Surf Avenue
Meyers, Rella—3796 Surf Avenue
Miller, Rosalie—3722 Lyme Avenue
Minoff, Marvin—3844 Lyme Avenue
Minton, Victor—4044 Highland Avenue
Murnick, Sharon—3738 Maple Avenue
Needle, Florence—3716 Oceanic Avenue
Needle, Irene—3716 Oceanic Avenue
Nevins, Alfred—3840 Lyme Avenue
Nevins, David—3840 Lyme Avenue
Oberfield, Elliot—3827 Oceanic Avenue
Oberfield, Richard—3827 Oceanic Avenue
Orans, Anita—4905 Surf Avenue
Ostrie, Barry—3774 Surf Avenue
Ostrie, Jeff—3774 Surf Avenue
Pierce, Ann—4606 Surf Avenue
Pincus, Eddie—3855 Lyme Avenue
Pincus, Elaine—3855 Lyme Avenue
Pinsker, Eleanor—3808 Maple Avenue
Plattman, Irwin—24 Tudor Terrace
Post, Richard—4504 Beach 45th Street
Powsner, Anna—3807 Laurel Avenue
Powsner, Lou—3807 Laurel Avenue
Purisch, Corrine—3723 Maple Avenue
Rabb, David—4504 Beach 45th Street

Rabb, Ethel—4504 Beach 45th Street
Radetsky, Alan—4020 Atlantic Avenue
Radetsky, Mona—4020 Atlantic Avenue
Rattner, Phyllis—3715 Sea Gate Avenue
Reinhard, Arthur—3764 Surf Avenue
Reis, Audrey—3822 Nautilus Avenue
Ricken, Grace—4111 Highland Avenue
Rifkin, Eugene—3829 Oceanic Avenue
Rifkin, Monroe—3829 Oceanic Avenue
Ringer, Robert—3736 Cypress Avenue
Rivlin, Orah—3916 Laurel Avenue
Rivlin, Ziev—3916 Laurel Avenue
Robins, Donald—3780 Surf Avenue
Rosen, Arnold—4016 Atlantic Avenue
Rosen, Harold—4016 Atlantic Avenue
Rosenberg, Stanley—3820 Lyme Avenue
Rosensweet, Eugene—3742 Maple Avenue
Rosensweet, Florence—3742 Maple Avenue
Rosenthal, Paul—3719 Poplar Avenue
Rosenzweig, Eli—4114 Highland Avenue
Rosenzweig, Roberta—4919 Surf Avenue
Rubel, Martin—4627 Beach 46th Street
Rubel, Renee—3821 Maple Avenue
Rubine, Phyllis—3740 Poplar Avenue
Rubine, Stanley—3740 Poplar Avenue
Rubinstein, Diana—4222 Surf Avenue
Rubinstein, Morton—3820 Lyme Avenue
Rubinstein, Richard—4810 Surf Avenue
Sadetsky, Flora—3840 Laurel Avenue
Sadetsky, Irwin—3840 Laurel Avenue
Sadetsky, Rose—3840 Laurel Avenue
Salzhauer, Charles—3815 Laurel Avenue
Sapon, Etta—3768 Surf Avenue
Schachter, Norman—3821 Laurel Avenue
Schindler, William—4048 Surf Avenue
Schneider, Jerome—3831 Lyme Avenue

Schonhaut, Leonard—3832 Laurel Avenue
Schwartz, Joan—3912 Cypress Avenue
Schwartz, Leonora—3907 Lyme Avenue
Schwartz, Noel—4314 Sea Gate Avenue
Schwartz, Norman—4024 Surf Avenue
Segal, Lenore—3804 Laurel Avenue
Seidon, Sheila—3722 Poplar Avenue
Seltzer, Rita—3712 Oceanic Avenue
Serper, Barry—3764 Surf Avenue
Shapiro, Maurice—3712 Poplar Avenue
Shapiro, Rhoda—3807 Oceanic Avenue
Sherman, Sheilah—3728 Maple Avenue
Shore, Donald—3821 Laurel Avenue
Shorofsky, Francine—4406 Beach 44th Street
Shorofsky, Morris—4406 Beach 44th Street
Shultz, Sheldon,—3812 Maple Avenue
Shurgrin, Denise—4401 Atlantic Avenue
Silver, Nina—4720 Beach 47th Street
Silverman, Ralph—3915 Laurel Avenue
Silverman, Sydelle—3915 Laurel Avenue
Simons, Miriam—3740 Lyme Avenue
Smith, Carol—4204 Highland Avenue
Sommer, Kenneth—3780 Surf Avenue
Soshtain, Isabelle—3802 Neptune Avenue
Sperber, Phyllis—3829 Laurel Avenue
Spinner, Joseph—3709 Nautilus Avenue
Spodek, Sheldon—3819 Nautilus Avenue
Spodek, Walter—3819 Neptune Avenue
Starkman, Elaine—3715 Lyme Avenue
Stein, Philip—4010 Highland Avenue
Steinberg, Gloria—3809 Maple Avenue
Steinklein, Sheila—3820 Laurel Avenue
Stern, Audrey—4307 Highland Avenue
Stern, Jack—4307 Highland Avenue
Stern, Jerry—3842 Neptune Avenue
Stone, Howard—3907 Sea Gate Avenue

Stone, Jerome—3907 Sea Gate Avenue
Stuchin, Geraldine—3826 Laurel Avenue
Sultan, Grace—3817 Maple Avenue
Sultan, Stephen—3817 Maple Avenue
Sussman, Belle—3725 Lyme Avenue
Sussman, Morton—3725 Lyme Avenue
Tankowitz, Martin—26 Tudor Terrace
Tankowitz, Shirley—26 Tudor Terrace
Tarnapol, Elaine—4115 Manhattan Avenue
Taylor, Audrey—3832 Lyme Avenue
Trupin, Harriet—4505 Surf Avenue
Trupin, Jacqueline—4505 Surf Avenue
Tucker, Marilyn—4010 Sea Gate Avenue
Wachs, Marilyn—3733 Lyme Avenue
Warshaw, Martha—4001 Sea Gate Avenue
Weinstein, Patricia—3768 Surf Avenue
Weiser, Lenore—3842 Maple Avenue
Weiser, Saul—4202 Manhattan Avenue
Weiss, Harvey—5020 Ocean View Avenue
Williams, Frank—3900 Neptune Avenue
Winter, Esther—3719 Lyme Avenue
Young, Iris—3734 Poplar Avenue
Young, Robert—3734 Popular Avenue
Zimmerman, Lucille—3786 Surf Avenue
Zorn, Anita—3829 Maple Avenue

INDEX

Symbols

Z